BANGA VAICEKAUSKIENĖ
YARNWAVE

CROCHET CATS & DOGS

15 amigurumi patterns for pet lovers

METEOOR BOOKS

Crochet Cats & Dogs
15 Amigurumi Patterns for Pet Lovers

Banga Vaicekauskienė (YarnWave)

Have you made characters with patterns from this book?
Share your creations on **www.amigurumi.com/5500**
or on Instagram with **#crochetcatsanddogs**

First published September 2025 by Meteoor BV, Antwerp, Belgium
www.meteoorbooks.com – hello@meteoorbooks.com

Printed and bound by Grafistar

ISBN 978-949164-357-6
D/2025/13.531/3

A catalogue record for this book is available from
the Royal Library of Belgium.

Hello and welcome!

I'm Banga, the creator and designer of the crocheted cats and dogs in this book.

My journey as an amigurumi designer began six years ago when I became a mom. When my daughter was born, I wanted to make something truly special for her – something crafted from the heart. That's when I created my very first design.

I quickly fell in love with creating my own amigurumi. Watching my ideas come to life as real plushies felt magical. What started off as a simple idea for my daughter grew into something I loved so much that I wanted to keep creating and sharing my designs with others.

This collection of cats and dogs is special to me, as I can't imagine life without my dog Lokis and my cat Luna. They bring so much happiness to my days, and I love having them around. Four-legged friends truly make life better.

This book is a dream come true, and I am beyond excited to share it with you. I hope these little crocheted friends bring you as much joy as they have brought me. Happy crocheting!

Banga

BASIC MATERIALS

Yarn

For every pattern in the book I've listed the materials used to create the design. I've used 100% cotton yarn for all of the cats and dogs, and for a few characters I've used it together with super fine mohair thread to create a fluffy texture. Don't feel tied to the choices of yarn fiber and thickness though: any weight of cotton, acrylic or wool can be used. Check the chart below for a quick comparison of yarn weights and corresponding recommended hook sizes.

> **Note:** *When crocheting amigurumi, you use a slightly smaller hook than what's recommended on the yarn label. This way, your stitches will be tighter and the stuffing will not show through.*

The patterns don't give the yarn quantity. The amount of yarn can vary according to your working tension and yarn thickness.

Fluffy mohair yarn

Mohair is a fiber from angora goats, which is generally spun with other fibers to create a fine and fluffy thread. For some amigurumi projects in this book, I suggest holding a mohair thread with cotton yarn to create a defined shape (thanks to the cotton) with an added soft "halo" effect (thanks to the mohair). When holding two yarns together, you may need a slightly bigger crochet hook to make your stitches more smoothly. To bring out the fluffiness of the mohair, you can comb the right side of the crochet work using a wire brush, moving the wire brush gently in all directions. Make sure to protect the safety eyes with a piece of washi tape while brushing around them.

Crochet hook

Hooks as well come in different sorts and sizes. Bigger hooks make bigger stitches than smaller ones. It's important to match the right hook size with the right weight of yarn. For amigurumi, you generally want to use a hook two or three sizes smaller than what's recommended on your yarn label. The crochet fabric should be quite tight, without any gaps through which the stuffing can escape. Using a smaller hook makes it easier to achieve this.

Hooks are usually made from aluminum or steel. Metal hooks tend to slip between the stitches more easily. Preferably choose a crochet hook with a rubber ergonomic handle.

Stitch marker

A stitch marker is a small metal or plastic clip (or safety pin). It's a simple tool to mark your starting point and give you the assurance that you've made the right number of stitches in each round. Mark the last stitch of the round with your stitch marker. You move your stitch marker up one round at the end of each round. When you reach your stitch marker after crocheting a new round, you take it out, crochet in this stitch,

NUMBER (SYMBOL)	1	2	3	4	5	6
CATEGORY NAME	super fine	fine	light	medium	heavy	very heavy
UK YARN TYPE	3 ply	4 ply	double knitting (DK)	aran	chunky	super chunky
US YARN TYPE	Fingering	Sport	Light Worsted	Worsted	Bulky	Extra Bulky
THE HOOK I RECOMMEND IN US SIZE	8 steel to B-1	B-1	B-1 to E-4	E-4 to 7	7 to I-9	I-9 to K-10 1/2
THE HOOK I RECOMMEND IN METRIC SIZE	1.5 to 2,5mm	2,5mm	2,5 to 3,5mm	3,5 to 4,5mm	4,5 to 5,5mm	5,5 to 6,5mm

then put it in the last stitch of the round you crocheted.

Stuffing

For the filling, polyester fiberfill is advised. It's washable and non-allergenic. The individual parts of a toy are stuffed while the piece is being crocheted. The stuffing of wider pieces such as the head or body begins when they are roughly half finished. For stuffing very thin pieces in which you cannot fit a finger, the back of a crochet hook or a chopstick can be used. Generally, when stuffing a toy, it's important to use more stuffing than you might initially think. If the toy is not stuffed tightly, it will lose its shape over time. On the other hand, if it's overstuffed, the stuffing may cause the fabric to stretch and become visible. You'll need to find the right balance.

Safety eyes

For most designs, safety eyes are used. Safety eyes come in two different parts – the front (the bead that will show on the outside, on a ribbed stem) and the back (the washer). The washer keeps the eye in place. Be careful when you apply safety eyes: once you put the washer on, you won't be able to pull it off again, so make sure that the post is where you want it to be before attaching the washer. If you choose to work with a different yarn weight than specified in the pattern, you may need to choose bigger or smaller safety eyes as well.

If you're crocheting these toys for children under the age of three, it is advised to embroider the facial features for safety.

TIP: It's helpful to mark the positions with pins before inserting the safety eyes, so you can adjust them if needed.

Tapestry needle

For embroidery, a tapestry needle with a rounded tip is used. This rounded tip makes it easier to insert your needle in a specific space without splitting your yarn.

Sewing pins

It can be handy to have some sewing pins lying around, to help position body parts before sewing them on permanently.

WHAT YOU SHOULD KNOW BEFORE YOU START

Skill level

easy ●○○ intermediate ●●○ advanced ●●●

Every pattern is marked with a skill level to indicate how easy they are to make. If this is your first time making amigurumi, it's best to start with an easy pattern and work up to the intermediate and advanced ones.

Pattern structure

These patterns are worked in **continuous spirals**. Crocheting in spirals can be confusing since there's no clear indication of where a new round begins and the previous one ends. To keep track of the rounds, you can mark the end of a round with a stitch marker. After crocheting the next round, you should end up right above your stitch marker. Move your stitch marker at the end of each round to keep track of where you are.

At the beginning of each line you will find '**Rnd + a number**' to indicate which round you are in. If a round is repeated, you'll read 'Rnd 9 – 12', for example. You then repeat this round four times, crocheting the stitches in round 9, 10, 11 and 12.

Although we usually crochet in rounds, occasionally it happens that we switch to **rows**, going back and forth instead of working in continuous spirals. When we switch to rows, it will be indicated with '**Row + a number**'. Turn your crochet work at the end of each row and start the next one following the instructions. When the next row starts with one or more turning chains, you do not count them as stitches.

At the end of each line you will find the number of stitches you should have in **square brackets**, for example [9]. When in doubt, take a moment to check your stitch count.

When parts of the instructions repeat throughout the round, we place them between **rounded brackets**, followed by the number of times this part should be worked. We do this to shorten the pattern and make it less cluttered.

V-stitches

All patterns in this book have been designed using regular V-shaped sc stitches (tutorial page 7). When crocheting with X-shaped sc stitches, the color work and the shaping might turn out a bit skewed. Using X-shaped sc stitches is therefore not recommended, as it would require adjusting parts of the patterns.

STITCH TUTORIALS

If this is your first time making amigurumi, you might find it useful to have a tutorial at hand. With the stitches explained on these pages, you can make all of the amigurumi in this book. We suggest you practice the basic stitches before you start making one of the designs. This will help you to read the patterns and abbreviations more comfortably, without having to browse back to these pages. This book is written in US crochet terms.

TUTORIAL VIDEOS

With each stitch explanation we have included a URL and QR code that will take you to our online stitch tutorial video, showing the technique step by step to help you master it even more quickly. Simply follow the link or scan the QR code with your smartphone. Phones with iOS will scan the QR code automatically in camera mode. For phones with Android you may need to install a QR Reader app first.

Scan or visit **www.stitch.show/ch** for the video tutorial

CHAIN (abbreviation: ch)

If you're working in rows, your first row will be a series of chain stitches.

Step 1: Use the hook to draw the yarn through the loop.

Step 2: Pull the loop until tight.

Step 3: Wrap the yarn over the hook from back to front. Pull the hook, carrying the yarn, through the loop already on your hook. You have now completed one chain stitch.

Step 4: Repeat these steps as indicated in the pattern to create a foundation chain.

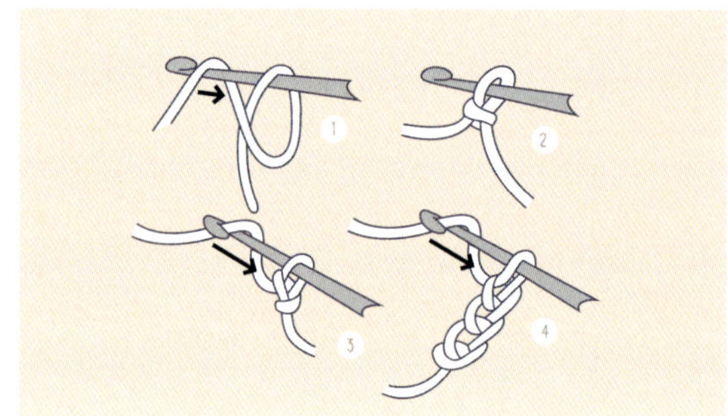

Scan or visit **www.stitch.show/FLO-BLO** for the video tutorial

INSERT THE HOOK (PLACEMENT OF STITCHES)

With the exception of chains, all crochet stitches require the hook to be inserted in existing stitches. Insert the hook underneath both top loops of the stitch in the row or round below. When inserting the hook, you take it from front to back through a stitch. The point of the hook must always look down or sideways, so the hook doesn't snag the yarn or the fabric. When asked to crochet FLO / BLO, you make the same stitch, though not in both loops.

Inserting the hook in front loops only (abbreviation: FLO)

When working in Front Loops Only, you pick up only the front loop toward you.

Inserting the hook in back loops only (abbreviation: BLO)

When working in Back Loops Only, you pick up only the back loop away from you.

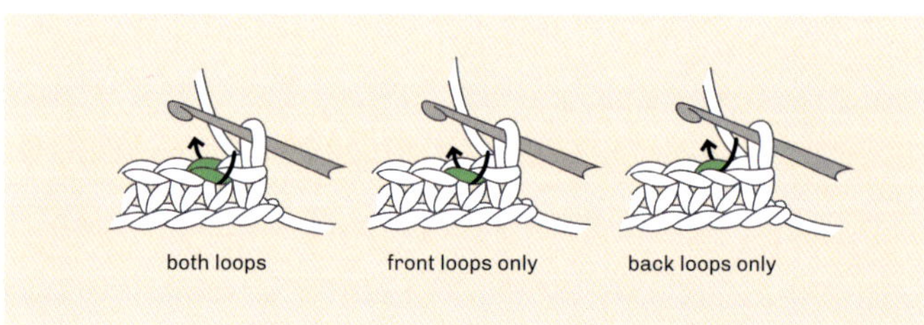

Scan or visit **www.stitch.show/slst** for the video tutorial

SLIP STITCH (abbreviation: slst)

A slip stitch is used to move across one or more stitches at once or to finish a piece.

Step 1: Insert your hook into the next stitch.

Step 2: Wrap the yarn over the hook and draw through the stitch and loop on your hook at once.

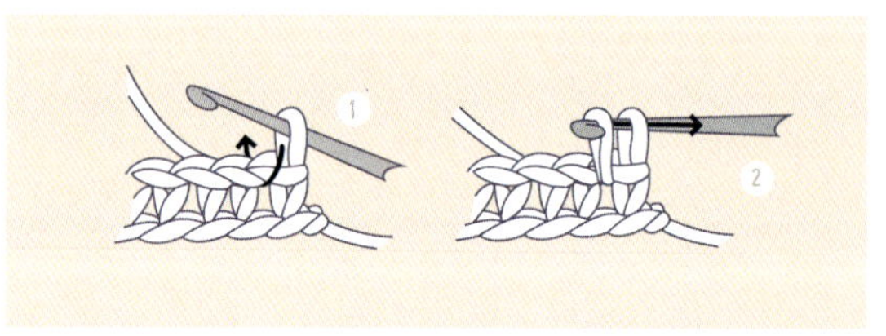

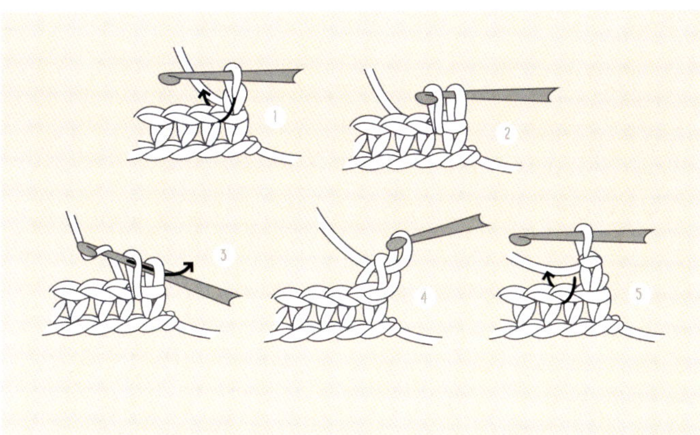

SINGLE CROCHET (abbreviation: sc)

Single crochet is the stitch that will be most frequently used in this book.

Step 1: Insert the hook into the next stitch.

Step 2: Wrap the yarn over the hook. Pull the yarn through the stitch. You will see that there are now two loops on the hook.

Step 3: Wrap the yarn over the hook again and draw it through both loops at once.

Step 4: You have now completed one single crochet.

Step 5: Insert the hook into the next stitch to continue.

Scan or visit **www.stitch.show/sc** for the video tutorial

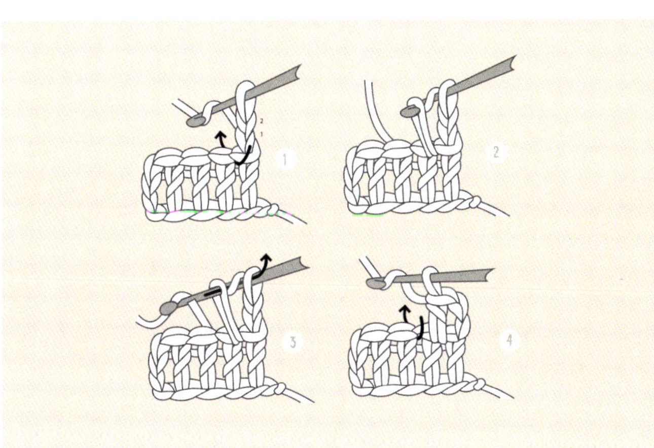

HALF DOUBLE CROCHET
(abbreviation: hdc)

Step 1: Bring your yarn over the hook from back to front before placing the hook in the stitch.

Step 2: Wrap the yarn over the hook and draw the yarn through the stitch. You now have three loops on the hook.

Step 3: Wrap the yarn over the hook again and pull it through all three loops on the hook. You have completed your first half double crochet.

Step 4: To continue, bring your yarn over the hook and insert it in the next stitch.

Scan or visit **www.stitch.show/hdc** for the video tutorial

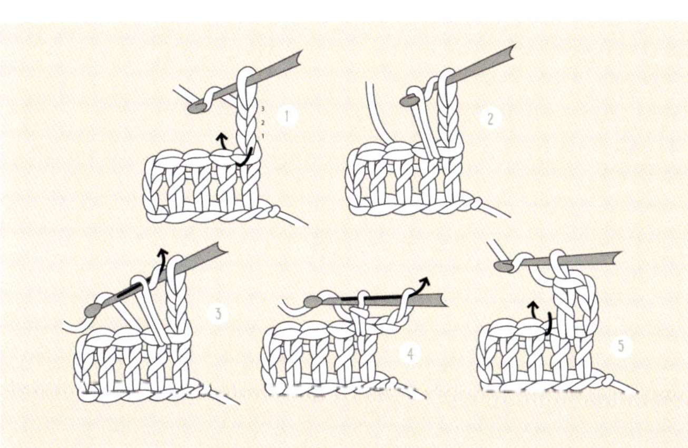

DOUBLE CROCHET (abbreviation: dc)

Step 1: Bring your yarn over the hook from back to front before placing the hook in the stitch.

Step 2: Wrap the yarn over the hook and draw the yarn through the stitch. You now have three loops on the hook.

Step 3: Wrap the yarn over the hook again and pull it through the first two loops on the hook. You now have two loops on the hook.

Step 4: Wrap the yarn over the hook one last time and draw it through both loops on the hook. You have now completed one double crochet.

Step 5: To continue, bring your yarn over the hook and insert it in the next stitch.

Scan or visit **www.stitch.show/dc** for the video tutorial

Scan or visit
www.stitch.show/inc
for the video tutorial

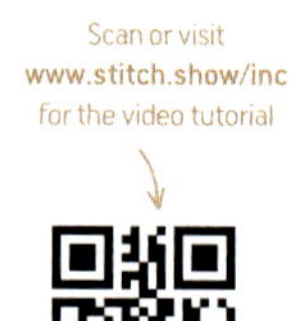

INCREASE (abbreviation: inc)

To increase, two single crochet stitches are made in the same stitch. This way, new stitches are created and the piece expands.

Step 1: Make a first single crochet stitch in the next stitch.

Step 2: Make a second single crochet stitch in the same stitch.

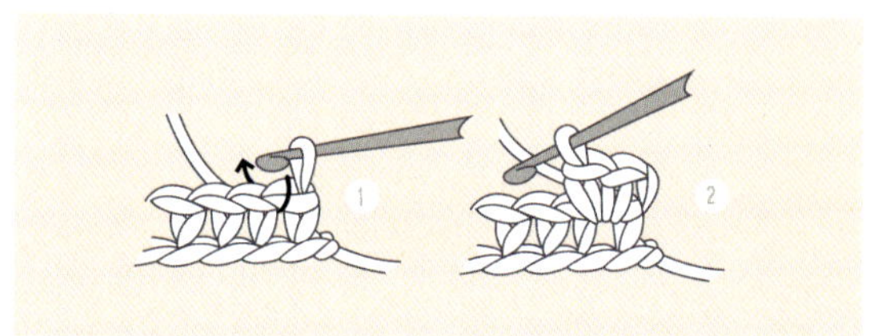

Note: *You can make an increase with any two stitches. The sample shows the basic increase with two single crochet stitches. You can also make an increase with 2 half double crochet stiches (hdc inc) or 2 double crochet stitches (dc inc).*

INVISIBLE DECREASE (abbreviation: dec)

When decreasing, two stitches are crocheted together. The number of stitches in a round therefore decreases and the piece shrinks.

Step 1: Insert the hook in the front loop of your first stitch. Now immediately insert your hook in the front loop of the second stitch. You now have three loops on your hook.

Step 2: Wrap the yarn over the hook and pull it through the first two loops on the hook.

Step 3: Wrap the yarn over the hook again and pull it through the remaining two loops on the hook. You have now completed one invisible decrease.

Scan or visit
www.stitch.show/dec
for the video tutorial

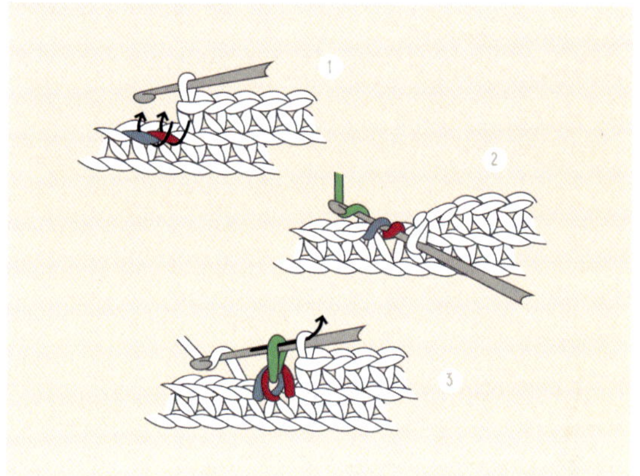

CROCHET AROUND A FOUNDATION CHAIN

Some pieces start with an oval. You make an oval by crocheting around a foundation chain.

Step 1: Crochet a foundation chain with as many chains as mentioned in the pattern and skip the first chain on the hook.

Step 2-3: Work a sc stitch in the next chain stitch. Work your crochet stitches into each chain across as mentioned in the pattern.

Step 4: The last stitch before turning is usually an increase stitch.

Step 5: Turn your work upside down to work into the underside of the chain stitches. You'll notice that only one loop is available, simply insert your hook in this loop. Work your stitches into each chain across.

Step 6: When finished, your last stitch should be next to the first stitch you made. You can now continue working in spirals.

Scan or visit
www.stitch.show/oval
for the video tutorial

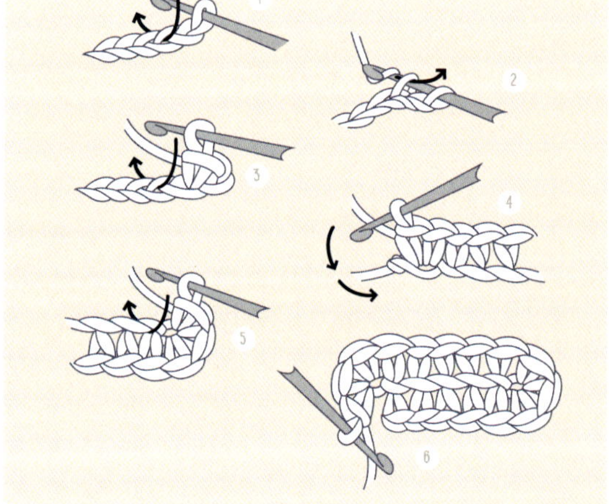

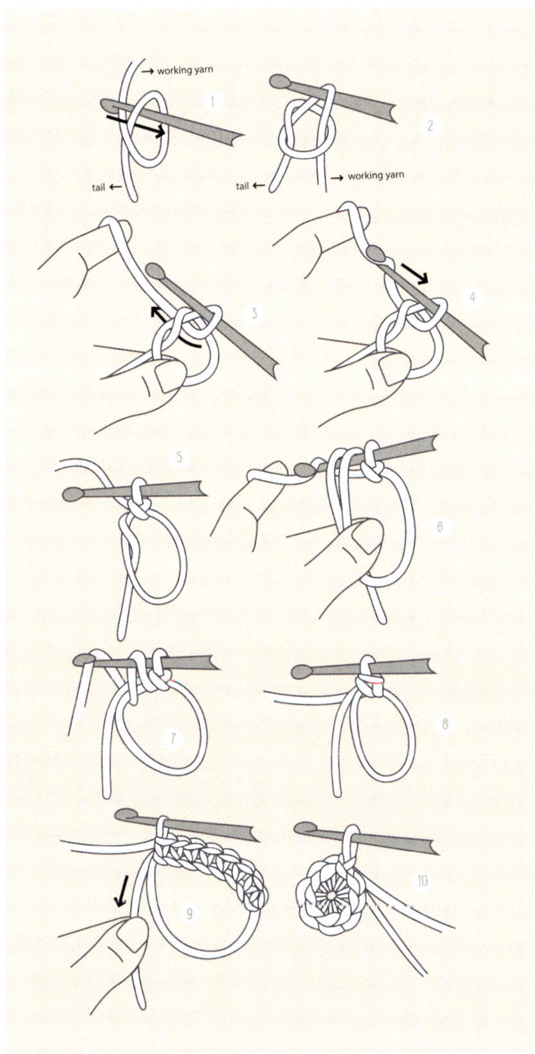

MAGIC RING

To start an amigurumi piece, you often need a little circle. A magic ring is the ideal way to start crocheting in the round as there will be no hole left in the middle of your starting round. You start by crocheting over an adjustable loop and finally pull the loop tight when you have finished the required number of stitches.

Step 1: Start with the yarn crossed to form a circle.

Step 2: Draw up a loop with your hook, but don't pull it tight.

Step 3: Hold the circle with your index finger and thumb and wrap the working yarn over your middle finger.

Step 4-5: Make one chain stitch by wrapping the yarn over the hook and pulling it through the loop on the hook.

Step 6: Now insert your hook into the circle and underneath the tail. Wrap the yarn over the hook and draw up a loop.

Step 7: Keep your hook above the circle and wrap the yarn over the hook again.

Step 8: Pull it through both loops on the hook. You have now completed your first single crochet stitch.
Continue to crochet (repeating step 6, 7, 8) until you have the required number of stitches as mentioned in the pattern.

Step 9-10: Now grab the yarn tail and pull to draw the center of the ring tightly.
You can now begin your second round by crocheting into the first single crochet stitch of the magic ring. You can use a stitch marker to remember where you started.

Scan or visit
www.stitch.show/magicring
for the video tutorial

Challenging? *You can try an alternative method, starting with 2 chain stitches. See the tutorial below.*

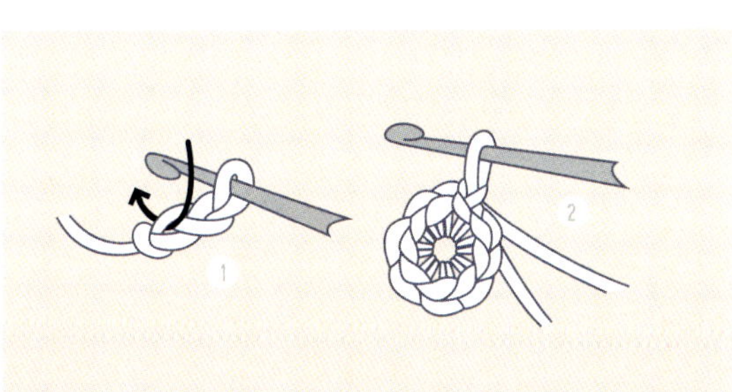

STARTING A CIRCULAR PIECE WITH 2 CHAIN STITCHES

If you don't want to use the magic ring technique, there's an easier way to start crocheting in the round. The downside of this technique is a tiny hole that remains visible in the center of the piece.

Step 1: Start by making a slip knot. Then, make 2 chain stitches and work x sc into the second chain from the hook – where x is the number of sc stitches you would make in your magic ring.

Step 2: Make a slst in the first stitch. You now have a little circle to start with.

Scan or visit
www.stitch.show/2ch
for the video tutorial

COLOR CHANGE – INVISIBLE COLOR CHANGE

When you want to switch from one color to the next, you work to within two stitches before a color change.

Step 1: Make the next single crochet stitch as usual, but don't pull the final loop through.

Step 2-3: Instead, wrap the new color of yarn around your hook and pull it through the remaining loops.

To make a neat color change, you can make the first stitch in the new color a slip stitch instead of a single crochet. Don't pull the slip stitch too tight or it will be difficult to crochet into in the next round. Tie the loose tails in a knot and leave them on the inside.

Scan or visit **www.stitch.show/colorchange** for the video tutorial

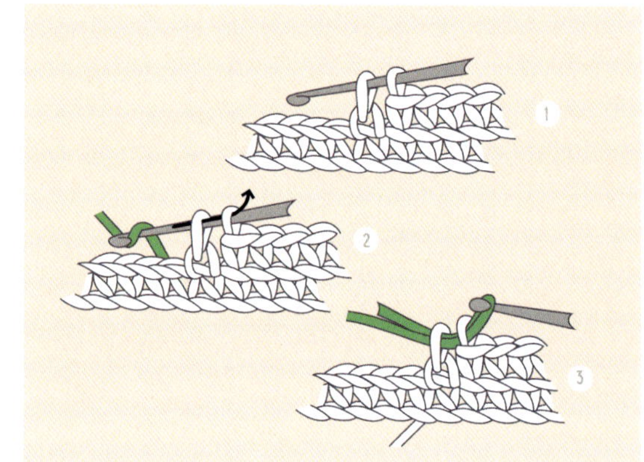

FASTENING OFF

Step 1: When you've finished crocheting, cut the yarn a couple of inches / cm from your last stitch. Pull the yarn through the last loop until it's all the way through. You now have a finished knot.

Step 2: Thread the long tail through a tapestry needle and insert it through the back loop of the next stitch. This way the finishing knot will remain invisible in your finished piece. You can use this yarn tail to continue sewing the pieces together.

Scan or visit **www.stitch.show/fastenoff** for the video tutorial

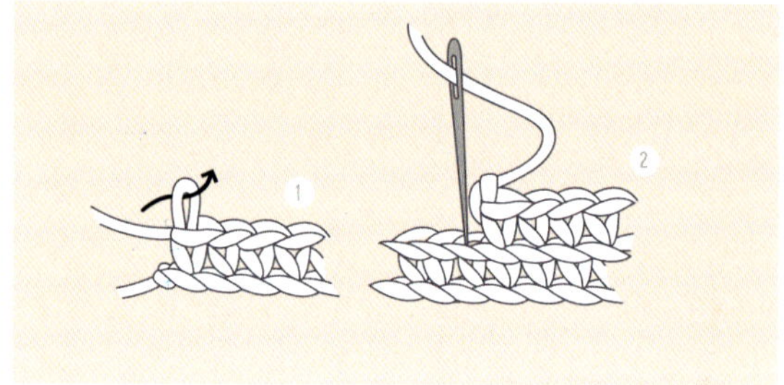

FASTENING OFF – INVISIBLE JOIN

Step 1: After completing the last stitch, cut your yarn, leaving a long yarn tail. Pull the yarn tail all the way through the stitch.

Step 2: Take the yarn tail on your tapestry needle. Insert your needle underneath both loops of the second stitch of the round, from front to back.

Step 3: Then insert it into the back loop only of the last stitch you made. Pull the tail to the back of the work and weave in the yarn end. You will see that your invisible join covers the first stitch of the round.

Scan or visit **www.stitch.show/fastenoff-invisible** for the video tutorial

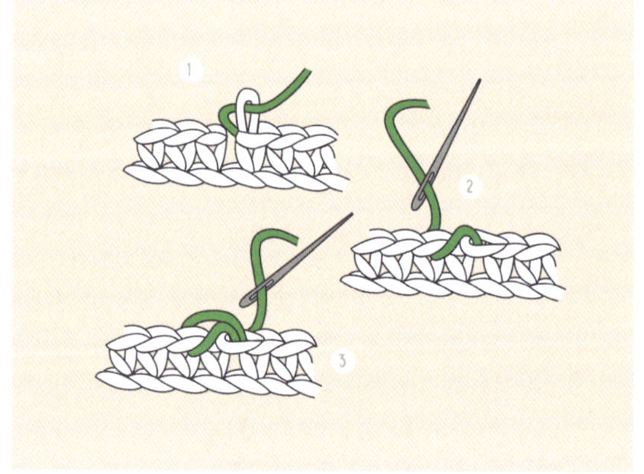

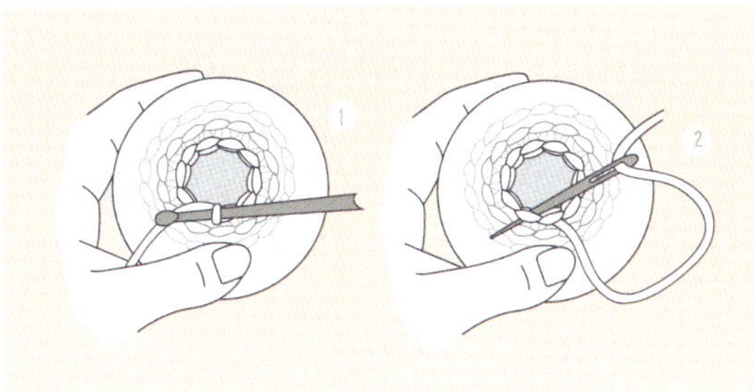

CLOSING OFF A PIECE

Step 1: After several decreases in the last round, a small hole will remain at the end of some pieces.

Step 2: Fasten off, leaving a long yarn tail. Thread the yarn tail left at the end of the piece onto a yarn needle, then insert the needle through each of the front loops of the stitches in the last round. Tighten and insert the needle through the nearest stitch, make a knot, and hide the yarn tail inside the piece.

Scan or visit **www.stitch.show/closing** for the video tutorial

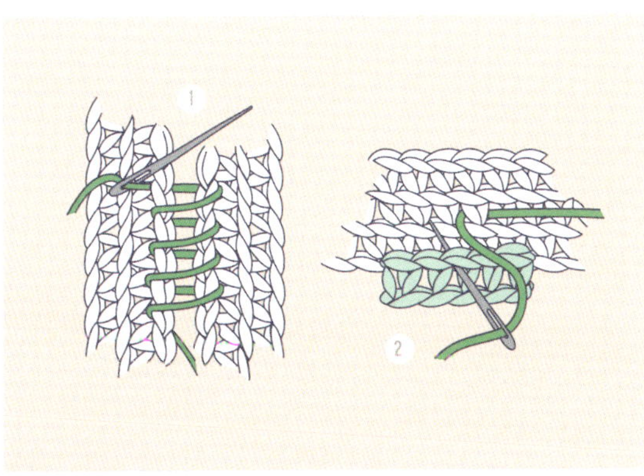

TIP: Always make sure the pieces are securely attached so that they can't be pulled off. Make small, neat stitches and try to make them show as little as possible.

JOINING PARTS – SEWING

First, pin the parts you want to sew to one another, so you can evaluate the result and adjust if necessary. If possible, use the leftover yarn tail from when you fastened off, or use a new length of the same yarn color of one of the pieces that you want to join.

Option 1 – When the different pieces are open: position the piece on the body and sew all around it, going through the stitches of both the extremity and the body.

Option 2 – When the opening of the different pieces is sewn closed before attaching them to the body: line up the stitches and sew through both loops of the open side and between the stitches of the closed side. Use the same yarn color as the pieces you want to join together.

Scan or visit **www.stitch.show/joining-sewing** for the video tutorial

Amigurumi gallery

With each pattern, we have included a URL and QR code that will take you to that character's dedicated online gallery. Share your finished amigurumi, find inspiration in the color and yarn choices of your fellow crocheters and enjoy the fun of crocheting.

Simply follow the link or scan the QR code with your mobile phone. Phones with iOS will scan the QR code automatically in camera mode. For phones with Android you may need to activate QR code scanning or install a separate QR Reader app.

Scan or visit www.amigurumi.com/5500 to share pictures and find inspiration.

MOLLY
the Beagle

Skill level: 
Size: 4.3" / 11 cm tall when made with the indicated yarn.

Amigurumi gallery: Scan or visit www.amigurumi.com/5501 to share pictures and find inspiration.

MATERIALS

- Sport weight yarn in orange, brown and white • B-1 / 2.25 mm crochet hook • Safety eyes (10 mm)
- Black and white embroidery thread • Yarn needle • Pins • Stitch markers • Fiberfill for stuffing
- Optional: Approx. 3.5" / 8 cm of wire or pipe cleaner *(for the tail if you want it to be posable)*
- Optional: White sewing thread *(for the assembly tip)*

HEAD (start in orange yarn)

Rnd 1: start 6 sc in a magic ring [6]

Rnd 2: inc in all 6 st [12]

Rnd 3: (sc in next st, inc in next st) repeat 6 times [18]

Rnd 4: (sc in next st, inc in next st, sc in next st) repeat 6 times [24]

Rnd 5: (sc in next 3 st, inc in next st) repeat 6 times [30]

Rnd 6: (sc in next 2 st, inc in next st, sc in next 2 st) repeat 6 times [36]

Rnd 7: (sc in next 5 st, inc in next st) repeat 6 times [42]

Rnd 8: (sc in next 3 st, inc in next st, sc in next 3 st) repeat 6 times [48]

Rnd 9 – 18: sc in all 48 st [48]

Rnd 19: (sc in next 3 st, dec, sc in next 3 st) repeat 6 times [42]

Rnd 20: (sc in next 5 st, dec) repeat 6 times [36]

In the next rounds, we'll alternate between orange and white yarn. The color change is indicated in italics.

Rnd 21: (sc in next 2 st, dec, sc in next 2 st) repeat 2 times, sc in next 2 st, dec, *(white)* sc in next 4 st, dec, sc in next 4 st, *(orange)* dec, sc in next 4 st, dec, sc in next 2 st [30]

The center of the white line made in round 21 is the middle of the puppy's face. Insert the safety eyes between rounds 14 and 15, with an interspace of 8 stitches 1.

Stuff the head with fiberfill and continue stuffing as you go.

Rnd 22: sc in next 4 st, dec, sc in next 4 st, *(white)* sc in next 4 st, dec, sc in next 8 st, dec, *(orange)* sc in next 4 st [27]

Rnd 23: sc in next 7 st, *(white)* sc in next 18 st, *(orange)* sc in next 2 st [27]

Rnd 24: sc in next 6 st, *(white)* sc in next 20 st, *(orange)* sc in next st [27]

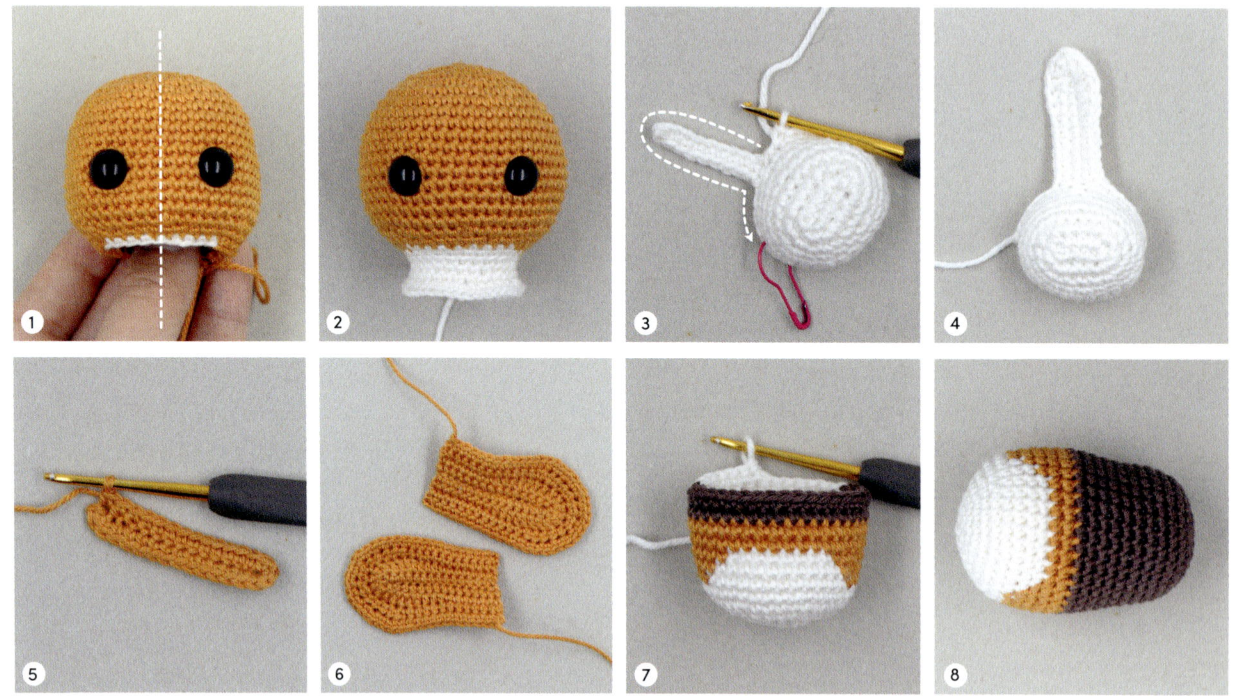

Rnd 25: sc in next 5 st, *(white)* sc in next 3 st, inc in next st, (sc in next 8 st, inc in next st) repeat 2 times [30]

Continue crocheting in white yarn.

Rnd 26: (sc in next 2 st, inc in next st, sc in next 2 st) repeat 6 times [36]

Rnd 27: sc in next 4 st [4] Leave the remaining stitches unworked.

Fasten off, leaving a yarn tail for sewing ❷.

SNOUT (in white yarn)

Leave a starting yarn tail. Ch 5. Stitches are worked around both sides of the foundation chain.

Rnd 1: start in second ch from hook, inc in this ch, sc in next 2 ch, 4 sc in last ch. Continue on the other side of the foundation chain, sc in next 2 ch, inc in last ch [12]

Rnd 2: inc in next 2 st, sc in next 2 st, inc in next 4 st, sc in next 2 st, inc in next 2 st [20]

Rnd 3: sc in all 20 st [20]

Using a yarn needle, weave the starting yarn tail through the foundation chain to hide the stitch gaps.

Rnd 4: (inc in next st, sc in next 4 st) repeat 4 times [24]

Rnd 5: sc in next 2 st, hdc in next st, hdc inc in next st, hdc in next 6 st, hdc inc in next st, hdc in next st, sc in next 12 st [26]

In the next round, we'll start making the stripe that covers the puppy's forehead.

Rnd 6: sc in next 3 st, hdc in next 10 st, sc in next 8 st, ch 11, start in second ch from hook, sc in next 10 ch, continue on the snout, skip next st, sc in next 4 st [35]

Rnd 7: sc in next 4 st, hdc in next 8 st, sc in next 9 st ❸, sc in next 7 st on the other side of the chains, hdc in next 2 st on the other side of the chains, dc in next st on the other side of the chain, 4 dc in the tip of the stripe, dc in next st, hdc in next 2 st, sc in next 7 st, continue on the snout, skip next st, sc in next 3 st [48]

Rnd 8: sc in next 3 st [3] Leave the remaining stitches unworked.

Fasten off, leaving a yarn tail for sewing ❹. Stuff the snout with fiberfill.

EAR (make 2, in orange yarn)

Ch 15. Stitches are worked around both sides of the foundation chain before switching to rows.

Row 1: start in second ch from hook, sc in next 13 ch, 4 sc in last ch. Continue on the other side of the foundation chain, sc in next 13 ch, ch 1, turn [30] 5

Row 2: sc in next 7 st, hdc in next 3 st, dc inc in next st, dc in next 3 st, dc inc in next 2 st, dc in next 3 st, dc inc in next st, hdc in next 3 st, sc in next 7 st, ch 1, turn [34]

Row 3: sc in next 12 st, hdc inc in next st, hdc in next 3 st, hdc inc in next 2 st, hdc in next 3 st, hdc inc in next st, sc in next 12 st, ch 1, turn [38]

Row 4: sc in next 13 st, (sc in next st, inc in next st) repeat 6 times, sc in next 13 st [44]

Fasten off, leaving a yarn tail for sewing 6. Shape the ears by gently stretching them outward.

BODY (start in white yarn)

Rnd 1: start 6 sc in a magic ring [6]

Rnd 2: inc in all 6 st [12]

Rnd 3: (sc in next st, inc in next st) repeat 6 times [18]

Rnd 4: (sc in next st, inc in next st, sc in next st) repeat 6 times [24]

Rnd 5: (sc in next 3 st, inc in next st) repeat 6 times [30]

Rnd 6: (sc in next 2 st, inc in next st, sc in next 2 st) repeat 6 times [36]

Rnd 7: sc in all 36 st [36]

In the next rounds, we'll alternate between white, orange and brown yarn. The color change is indicated in italics.

Rnd 8: sc in next 6 st, *(orange)* sc in next 6 st, *(white)* sc in next 12 st, *(orange)* sc in next 6 st, *(white)* sc in next 6 st [36]

Rnd 9: sc in next 6 st, *(orange)* sc in next 7 st, *(white)* sc in next 10 st, *(orange)* sc in next 7 st, *(white)* sc in next 6 st [36]

Rnd 10: sc in next 5 st, *(orange)* sc in next 9 st, *(white)* sc in

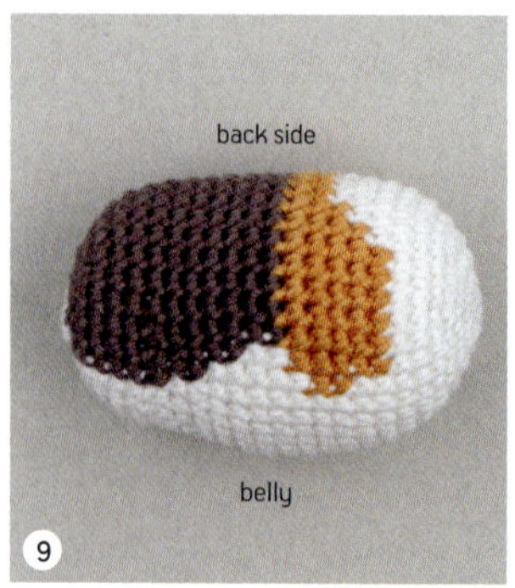

9

10

11

12

next 8 st, *(orange)* sc in next 9 st, *(white)* sc in next 5 st [36]
Rnd 11: sc in next 5 st, *(orange)* sc in next 26 st, *(white)* sc in next 5 st [36]
Rnd 12: sc in next 6 st, *(orange)* sc in next 24 st, *(white)* sc in next 6 st [36]
Rnd 13 – 14: sc in next 7 st, *(brown)* sc in next 22 st, *(white)* sc in next 7 st [36] 7
Sc in next st. This is the new start of the round.
Rnd 15 – 16: sc in next 7 st, *(brown)* sc in next 22 st, *(white)* sc in next 7 st [36]
Rnd 17: dec, sc in next 4 st, *(brown)* dec, sc in next 22 st, *(white)* dec, sc in next 4 st [33]
Stuff the body with fiberfill and continue stuffing as you go.
Rnd 18: sc in next 3 st, dec, *(brown)* sc in next 21 st, dec, *(white)* sc in next 3 st, dec [30]
Rnd 19: sc in next 4 st, *(brown)* sc in next 20 st, hdc in next 3 st, *(white)* hdc in next 3 st [30]
Rnd 20: hdc in next 4 st, *(brown)* hdc in next 2 st, sc in next 21 st, *(white)* sc in next 3 st [30]
Rnd 21: sc in next 5 st, *(brown)* sc in next 22 st, *(white)* sc in next 3 st [30]
Sc in next st. This is the new start of the round.
Rnd 22: sc in next 5 st, *(brown)* sc in next 21 st, *(white)* sc in next 4 st [30]
Rnd 23: dec, sc in next 3 st, *(brown)* (dec, sc in next 3 st) repeat 4 times, sc in next st, *(white)* dec, sc in next 2 st [24]
Rnd 24: sc in next st, dec, sc in next st, *(brown)* (sc in next st, dec, sc in next st) repeat 4 times, sc in next st, *(white)* dec, sc in next st [18]
Rnd 25: sc in next st, dec, *(brown)* (sc in next st, dec) repeat 4 times, sc in next st, *(white)* dec [12]
Rnd 26: dec 6 times [6]
Fasten off, leaving a yarn tail. Using a yarn needle, weave the yarn tail through the front loop of each remaining stitch and pull it tight to close 8 9.

FRONT LEG (make 2, start in white yarn)

Rnd 1: start 6 sc in a magic ring [6]
Rnd 2: (sc in next st, inc in next st) repeat 3 times [9]
Rnd 3: sc in next 4 st, inc in next st, sc in next 4 st [10]
Rnd 4 – 5: sc in all 10 st [10]
Rnd 6: sc in next 9 st, inc in next st [11]
In the next 2 rounds, we'll alternate between orange and white yarn. The color change is indicated in italics.
Rnd 7: sc in next 4 st, *(orange)* sc in next st, inc in next st, sc in next st, *(white)* sc in next 4 st [12]
Rnd 8: sc in next 3 st, *(orange)* sc in next 9 st [12]
Continue in orange yarn.
Rnd 9: sc in next 11 st, ch 1, turn [11] Leave the remaining stitch unworked.
Continue crocheting in rows.
Row 10: skip first sc, sc in next 7 st, ch 1, turn [7] Leave the remaining stitches unworked.
Row 11: skip first sc, sc in next 6 st, ch 1, turn [6]
Row 12: skip first sc, sc in next st, hdc in next st, dc inc in next st, hdc in next st, sc in next st [6]
Fasten off, leaving a yarn tail for sewing. Stuff the front legs with fiberfill 10.

HIND LEG (make 2)

Upper part (in orange yarn)
Rnd 1: start 7 sc in a magic ring [7]
Rnd 2: inc in all 7 st [14]
Rnd 3: (sc in next st, inc in next st) repeat 7 times [21]
Rnd 4: (sc in next st, inc in next st, sc in next st) repeat 7 times [28]
Rnd 5: (sc in next 3 st, inc in next st) repeat 7 times [35]
Rnd 6: sc in all 35 st [35]
Rnd 7: (sc in next 3 st, dec) repeat 7 times [28]
Rnd 8: (sc in next st, dec, sc in next st) repeat 7 times [21]
Stuff lightly with fiberfill. The upper part of the leg should have some volume, but also remain quite flat.
Rnd 9: (sc in next st, dec) repeat 7 times [14]
Rnd 10: dec 7 times [7]
Fasten off, leaving a yarn tail. Using a yarn needle, weave the yarn tail through the front loop of each remaining stitch and pull it tight to close. Leave a yarn tail for sewing.

Foot (in white yarn)
Rnd 1: start 6 sc in a magic ring [6]
Rnd 2: (sc in next st, inc in next st) repeat 3 times [9]
Rnd 3: sc in next 4 st, inc in next st, sc in next 4 st [10]
Rnd 4: sc in all 10 st, ch 1, turn [10]
Continue crocheting in rows.
Row 5: skip first sc, sc in next 6 st, ch 1, turn [6] Leave the remaining stitches unworked.
Row 6: skip first sc, sc in next st, hdc in next st, dc inc in next st, hdc in next st, sc in next st [6]
Fasten off, leaving a yarn tail for sewing. Stuff the feet with fiberfill 11.

13
14
15
16
17
18
right side up
19
attach the ears here
20
21
22
23
24
25
26
27

TAIL (start in white yarn)
Rnd 1: start 6 sc in a magic ring [6]
Rnd 2: sc in all 6 st [6]
Rnd 3: sc in next 5 st, inc in next st [7]
Rnd 4: sc in all 7 st [7]
Rnd 5: sc in next 3 st, inc in next st, sc in next 3 st [8]
Rnd 6: sc in all 8 st [8]
Change to brown yarn.
Rnd 7: sc in next 7 st, inc in next st [9]
Rnd 8: sc in next 4 st, inc in next st, sc in next 4 st [10]
Rnd 9 – 14: sc in all 10 st [10]
Rnd 15: sc in next 4 st, dec, sc in next 4 st [9]
Rnd 16: sc in all 9 st, ch 1, turn [9]
Continue crocheting in rows.
Row 17: skip first sc, sc in next 5 st, ch 1, turn [5] Leave the remaining stitches unworked.
Row 18: skip first sc, sc in next 4 st, ch 1, turn [4]
Row 19: skip first sc, sc in next 3 st [3]
Fasten off, leaving a long tail for sewing 12.

ASSEMBLY

TIP: Sewing white pieces onto the orange parts can be challenging. To make the seams less noticeable, try using white sewing thread and a thin needle instead of the yarn tails.

Assemble the eyes

- Using several strands of white thread, embroider a line along the outer edge of each eye.
- Using black thread, embroider the upper outline 13.

Attach the snout

- Pin the snout in place just below the safety eyes, aligning the stripe with the center of the forehead. Sew it on using the remaining yarn tail, but don't weave in the end yet 14.
- Using the same yarn tail, close any gaps between the snout and the forehead stripe 15.

Embroider the nose

- Using a strand of black embroidery thread, embroider the nose on the top side of the snout, on rounds 2-3, aligned with the forehead stripe 16.

Attach the ears

- Position the ears on both sides of the head, between rounds 5-13 17 18, with the right side facing upward 19. Pin them in place and sew them on using the remaining yarn tails.
- Bend the ears down and sew them to the face to secure the position 20.

Attach the front legs

- Place the front legs on the front side of the body, on rounds 6-12. They should be aligned with the orange parts of the body. Pin them in place and check to see if the puppy can sit properly. Adjust the position if needed and sew around using the remaining yarn tails 21 22.

Attach the hind legs

- Place the upper parts of the hind legs on the lower sides of the body. It's easiest to do this while your dog is sitting on a flat surface. The upper parts should cover rounds 16-23 of the body. Pin them in place and sew around using the remaining yarn tails 23 24.
- Place the feet below the upper parts of the hind legs. The feet should be facing the front side of the dog. Pin them in place and sew around using the remaining yarn tails 25 26.

Attach the tail

- If you want the tail to be posable, insert the wire or pipe cleaner. Otherwise, lightly stuff it with fiberfill.
- Position the tail to the back of the body, with the tail pointing to the same side you want your dog to look at. Pin it in place and sew around using the remaining yarn tail 27.
- Slightly bend the tail to the side.

Attach the head

- Place the head on top of the body. Turn the head slightly to the side (in the same direction as the tail) to give your dog a cuter look. Pin it in place and sew around using the remaining yarn tail.

WILLOW
the British Shorthair

Skill level: ● ○ ○
Size: 6.3" / 16 cm tall (playful cat) or 2.8" / 7 cm tall (sleeping cat) when made with the indicated yarn.

Amigurumi gallery: Scan or visit www.amigurumi.com/5502 to share pictures and find inspiration.

MATERIALS

• Sport weight yarn in dark gray • B-1 / 2.25 mm crochet hook • Safety eyes (12 mm) • Light gray sewing thread *(for the whiskers)* • Black and mustard yellow embroidery thread • Yarn needle • Pins • Stitch markers • Fiberfill for stuffing • Optional: approx. 4" / 10 cm of wire or pipe cleaner *(for the tail if you want it to be posable)* • Optional: super fine weight mohair yarn in dark gray *(if you decide to crochet using two strands of yarn)*

NOTE

To achieve the soft texture shown in the photos, I crocheted with two strands held together: one strand of sport weight cotton and one strand of super fine weight mohair in a matching color. This is completely optional, using a single strand of yarn works just as well.

Follow the main instructions to make a playful cat. If you would like to make the sleeping cat instead, be sure to read the additional instructions on page 27 first.

HEAD (in dark gray yarn)
Rnd 1: start 6 sc in a magic ring [6]
Rnd 2: inc in all 6 st [12]
Rnd 3: (sc in next st, inc in next st) repeat 6 times [18]
Rnd 4: (sc in next st, inc in next st, sc in next st) repeat 6 times [24]
Rnd 5: (sc in next 3 st, inc in next st) repeat 6 times [30]
Rnd 6: (sc in next 2 st, inc in next st, sc in next 2 st) repeat 6 times [36]
Rnd 7: (sc in next 5 st, inc in next st) repeat 6 times [42]
Rnd 8: (sc in next 3 st, inc in next st, sc in next 3 st) repeat 6 times [48]
Rnd 9 – 15: sc in all 48 st [48]
Rnd 16: (sc in next 3 st, dec, sc in next 3 st) repeat 6 times [42]
Rnd 17: (sc in next 5 st, dec) repeat 6 times [36]
Insert the safety eyes between rounds 13 and 14, with an interspace of 8 stitches. Stuff the head with fiberfill and continue stuffing as you go.
Rnd 18: (sc in next 2 st, dec, sc in next 2 st) repeat 6 times [30]
Rnd 19: (sc in next 3 st, dec) repeat 6 times [24]
Rnd 20: (sc in next st, dec, sc in next st) repeat 6 times [18]
Rnd 21: (sc in next st, dec) repeat 6 times [12]

Rnd 22: dec 6 times [6]

Fasten off, leaving a yarn tail. Using a yarn needle, weave the yarn tail through the front loop of each remaining stitch and pull it tight to close. Weave in the yarn end ①.

RIGHT EAR (in dark gray yarn)

Ch 2. Crochet in rows.

Row 1: start in second ch from hook, inc in this ch, ch 1, turn [2]

Row 2: sc in next st, inc in next st, ch 1, turn [3]

Row 3: sc in next 2 st, inc in next st, ch 2, turn [4]

Row 4: dc inc in next st, hdc in next st, sc in next 2 st, ch 1, turn [5]

Row 5: sc in next 3 st, hdc in next st, dc inc in next st, ch 2, turn [6]

Row 6: dc inc in next st, dc in next st, hdc inc in next st, sc in next 3 st [8]

Next, we crochet around the ear ②.

Row 7: ch 1, turn, sc in next 7 st, 3 sc in next st, continue in the row-ends on the longer side of the ear, sc in next 8 st, 3 sc in next st, continue in the row-ends on the shorter side of the ear, sc in next 5 st, inc in next st, ch 1, turn [28] ③

Row 8: sc in next 20 st [20] Leave the remaining stitches unworked.

Fasten off, leaving a yarn tail for sewing.

LEFT EAR (in dark gray yarn)

Ch 2. Crochet in rows.

Row 1: start in second ch from hook, inc in this ch, ch 1, turn [2]

Row 2: sc in next st, inc in next st, ch 1, turn [3]

Row 3: sc in next 2 st, inc in next st, ch 1, turn [4]

Row 4: sc in next 2 st, hdc in next st, dc inc in next st, ch 2, turn [5]

Row 5: dc inc in next st, hdc in next st, sc in next 3 st, ch 1, turn [6]

Row 6: sc in next 3 st, hdc inc in next st, dc in next st, dc inc in next st [8]

Next, we crochet around the ear.

Row 7: ch 1, turn, sc in next 7 st, 3 sc in next st, continue in the row-ends on the shorter side of the ear, sc in next 5 st, 3 sc in next st, continue in the row-ends on the longer side of the ear, sc in next 8 st, inc in next st, ch 1, turn [28]

Row 8: sc in next 20 st [20] Leave the remaining stitches unworked.

Fasten off, leaving a yarn tail for sewing ④.

SNOUT (in dark gray yarn)

Leave a starting yarn tail. Ch 4. Stitches are worked around both sides of the foundation chain.

Rnd 1: start in second ch from hook, inc in this ch, sc in next ch, 4 sc in last ch. Continue on the other side of the foundation chain, sc in next ch, inc in next ch [10]

Rnd 2: inc in next 2 st, sc in next st, inc in next 4 st, sc in next st, inc in next 2 st [18]

Rnd 3: sc in all 18 st [18]

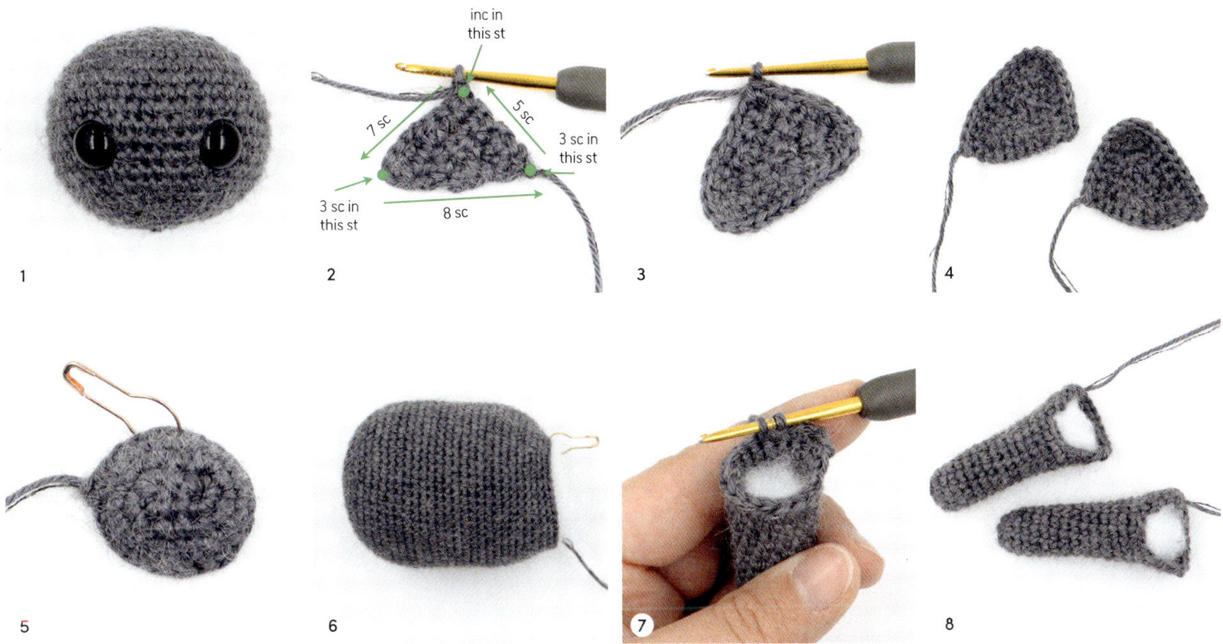

1 2 3 4 5 6 7 8

Using a yarn needle, weave the starting yarn tail through the foundation chain to hide the stitch gaps.

Rnd 4: sc in next 2 st, hdc inc in next st, dc in next 4 st, hdc inc in next st, sc in next 7 st *(mark the last sc with a stitch marker)*, sc in next 3 st [20]

Rnd 5: sc in next 2 st [2] Leave the remaining stitches unworked.

Fasten off, leaving a yarn tail for sewing 5.

Attach the whiskers

Prepare 4 strands of light gray sewing thread, each about 6" / 15 cm long. Note that the marked stitch indicates the top center of the snout. With the wrong side of the snout facing you, tie 2 strands on the left and 2 strands on the right, keeping the knots on the inside so they remain hidden from the front. Each knot creates 2 loose ends, giving you 4 strands on each side. Pull each strand through a separate stitch gap to the front side of the snout.

BODY (in dark gray yarn)

Rnd 1: start 7 sc in a magic ring [7]

Rnd 2: inc in all 7 st [14]

Rnd 3: (sc in next st, inc in next st) repeat 7 times [21]

Rnd 4: (sc in next st, inc in next st, sc in next st) repeat 7 times [28]

Rnd 5: (sc in next 3 st, inc in next st) repeat 7 times [35]

Rnd 6: (sc in next 2 st, inc in next st, sc in next 2 st) repeat 7 times [42]

Rnd 7: (sc in next 5 st, inc in next st) repeat 7 times [49]

Rnd 8: (sc in next 3 st, inc in next st, sc in next 3 st) repeat 7 times [56]

Rnd 9: (sc in next 13 st, inc in next st) repeat 4 times [60]

Rnd 10 – 27: sc in all 60 st [60]

Stuff the body with fiberfill and continue stuffing as you go.

Rnd 28: sc in next 12 st, (sc in next 5 st, dec, sc in next 5 st) repeat 4 times [56]

Rnd 29: sc in next 12 st, (sc in next 9 st, dec) repeat

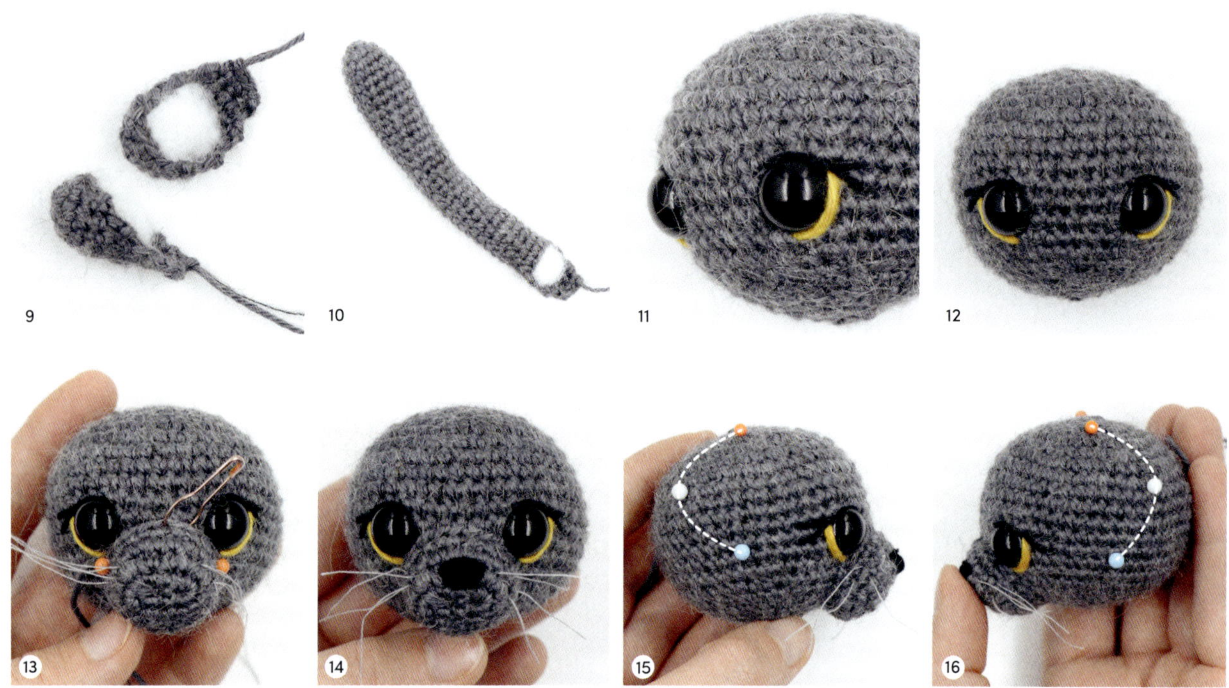
9 10 11 12 13 14 15 16

4 times [52]

Rnd 30: sc in next 12 st, (sc in next 4 st, dec, sc in next 4 st) repeat 4 times [48]

Rnd 31: sc in next 12 st, (sc in next 7 st, dec) repeat 4 times [44]

Sc in next st. This is the new start of the round.

Rnd 32: sc in next 12 st, (sc in next 3 st, dec, sc in next 3 st) repeat 4 times [40]

Rnd 33: sc in next 12 st, (sc in next 5 st, dec) repeat 2 times *(mark the last stitch with a stitch marker)*, (sc in next 5 st, dec) repeat 2 times [36]

Fasten off, leaving a yarn tail for sewing 6.

FRONT LEG (make 2, in dark gray yarn)

Rnd 1: start 6 sc in a magic ring [6]

Rnd 2: inc in all 6 st [12]

Rnd 3 – 10: sc in all 12 st [12]

Stuff the front leg with fiberfill and continue stuffing as you go.

Rnd 11: sc in next 11 st, inc in next st [13]

Rnd 12: sc in next 6 st, inc in next st, sc in next 6 st [14]

Rnd 13: sc in next 13 st, inc in next st [15]

Rnd 14: sc in next 7 st, inc in next st, sc in next 7 st [16]

Rnd 15: sc in next 15 st, inc in next st [17]

Rnd 16: sc in next 8 st, inc in next st, sc in next 8 st, ch 1, turn [18]

Continue crocheting in rows.

Row 17: skip first sc, sc in next 14 st, ch 1, turn [14] Leave the remaining stitches unworked 7.

Row 18: skip first sc, sc in next 13 st, ch 1, turn [13]

Row 19: skip first sc, sc in next 12 st [12]

Fasten off, leaving a yarn tail for sewing 8.

HIND LEG (make 2, in dark gray yarn)

Rnd 1: start 6 sc in a magic ring [6]

Rnd 2: inc in all 6 st [12]

Rnd 3: sc in all 12 st, ch 1, turn [12]

Continue crocheting in rows.

Row 4: skip first sc, sc in next 9 st, ch 1, turn [9] Leave the

remaining stitches unworked.

Row 5: skip first sc, sc in next 8 st, ch 1, turn [8]
Row 6: skip first sc, sc in next 7 st, ch 1, turn [7]
Row 7: skip first sc, sc in next 6 st, ch 1, turn [6]
Row 8: skip first sc, sc in next 5 st, ch 1, turn [5]
Row 9: skip first sc, sc in next 4 st, ch 1, turn [4]
Row 10: skip first sc, sc in next 3 st [3]
Fasten off, leaving a yarn tail for sewing. Stuff the hind leg with fiberfill 9.

TAIL (in dark gray yarn)

Rnd 1: start 6 sc in a magic ring [6]
Rnd 2: inc in all 6 st [12]
Rnd 3: (sc in next 3 st, inc in next st) repeat 3 times [15]
Rnd 4 – 8: sc in all 15 st [15]
Rnd 9: sc in next 13 st, dec [14]
If you want the tail to be posable, insert the wire or pipe cleaner. Otherwise, lightly stuff it with fiberfill.
Rnd 10 – 12: sc in all 14 st [14]
Rnd 13: sc in next 6 st, dec, sc in next 6 st [13]
Rnd 14 – 16: sc in all 13 st [13]
Rnd 17: sc in next 11 st, dec [12]
Rnd 18 – 20: sc in all 12 st [12]
Rnd 21: sc in next 5 st, dec, sc in next 5 st [11]
Rnd 22 – 29: sc in all 11 st [11]
Rnd 30: sc in all 11 st, ch 1, turn [11]
Continue crocheting in rows.
Row 31: skip first sc, sc in next 6 st, ch 1, turn [6] Leave the remaining stitches unworked.
Row 32: skip first sc, sc in next 5 st, ch 1, turn [5]
Row 33: skip first sc, sc in next 4 st, ch 1, turn [4]
Row 34: skip first sc, sc in next 3 st, ch 1, turn [3]
Row 35: skip first sc, sc in next 2 st [2]
Fasten off, leaving a yarn tail for sewing 10.

ASSEMBLY

Make the eyes colorful

- Using several strands of mustard yellow thread, embroider a line along the outer edge of each eye 11.

- Using black thread, embroider the upper outline and eyelashes 11 12.

Attach the snout

- Position the snout just below the eyes, with the stitch marker centered between them 13. Pin the snout in place, remove the stitch marker and sew around using the remaining yarn tail. Stuff the snout with fiberfill before closing the seam.
- Using black thread, embroider a nose on round 2 of the top side of the snout.
- Cut the whiskers to the desired length. You get the cutest look when each whisker is a slightly different length 14.

Attach the ears

- Position the ears on both sides of the head, between rounds 3-14 15 16. Pin them in place and sew them on using the remaining yarn tails 17.

Attach the head to the body

- Place the head on the body with the body's stitch marker aligned with the top of the head. The body covers rounds 5-16 at the back of the head 18 19. Pin the body in place and sew around using the remaining yarn tail.

Attach the front legs

- Place the front legs on the neck seam, right below the ears. The longer edges of the legs should face outward. Pin them in place and sew around using the remaining yarn tails 20 21.
- Take a strand of dark gray yarn and sew the paws to the sides of the snout, right below the whiskers 22 23.

Attach the hind legs

- Place the hind legs on both sides of the body. It's easiest to do this while your cat is lying on a flat surface. The legs should cover rounds 11-19 and there should be an inter-space of 11 stitches between them. Pin them in place and sew around using the remaining yarn tails. If needed, add more stuffing before closing the seam 24 25.

Attach the tail

- Attach the tail to the back of the body, aligning the opening to cover rounds 5 to 11, with the tail pointing upward. Pin it in place and sew around using the remaining yarn tail.
- Slightly bend the tail to the side to give your cat a cuter look.

How to change your cat into a sleeping cat

- Instead of using safety eyes, you embroider closed eyes with black thread on rounds 12-13 of the head, spacing them 6 stitches apart 26.
- Make only one hind leg.
- Position the tail pointing toward the side without the hind leg, and sew it to the cat's side to secure it in place 27 28.

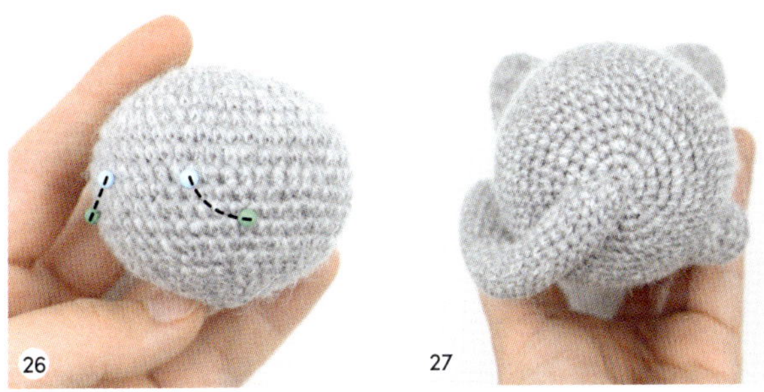

26 27

28

SOPHIE
the Cat in a Sweater

Skill level: 
Size: 6" / 15 cm tall when made with the indicated yarn.

Amigurumi gallery: Scan or visit www.amigurumi.com/5503 to share pictures and find inspiration.

MATERIALS

• Sport weight yarn in brown, white, teal and pink • B-1 / 2.25 mm crochet hook • Safety eyes (10 mm) • White sewing thread *(for the whiskers)* • Black, pink and blue embroidery thread • Yarn needle • Pins • Stitch markers • Fiberfill for stuffing • Optional: approx. 4" / 10 cm of wire or pipe cleaner *(for the tail if you want it to be posable)* • Optional: super fine weight mohair yarn in brown, white, teal and pink *(if you decide to crochet using two strands of yarn)*

NOTE

To achieve the soft texture shown in the photos, I crocheted with two strands held together: one strand of sport weight cotton and one strand of super fine weight mohair in a matching color. This is completely optional, using a single strand of yarn works just as well.

HEAD (start in brown yarn)

Rnd 1: start 6 sc in a magic ring [6]

Rnd 2: inc in all 6 st [12]

Rnd 3: (sc in next st, inc in next st) repeat 6 times [18]

Rnd 4: (sc in next st, inc in next st, sc in next st) repeat 6 times [24]

Rnd 5: (sc in next 3 st, inc in next st) repeat 6 times [30]

Rnd 6: (sc in next 2 st, inc in next st, sc in next 2 st) repeat 6 times [36]

Rnd 7: (sc in next 5 st, inc in next st) repeat 6 times [42]

Rnd 8: (sc in next 3 st, inc in next st, sc in next 3 st) repeat 6 times [48]

Rnd 9 – 11: sc in all 48 st [48]

In the next round, we'll alternate between brown and white yarn. The color change is indicated in italics.

Rnd 12 – 13: sc in next 20 st, *(white)* sc in next 2 st, *(brown)* sc in next 5 st, *(white)* sc in next 2 st, *(brown)* sc in next 19 st [48]

Rnd 14 – 18: sc in all 48 st [48]

Rnd 19: (sc in next 3 st, dec, sc in next 3 st) repeat 6 times [42]

Insert the safety eyes between rounds 14 and 15, with an interspace of 8 stitches. The white patches on the head are positioned just above and slightly between the eyes.

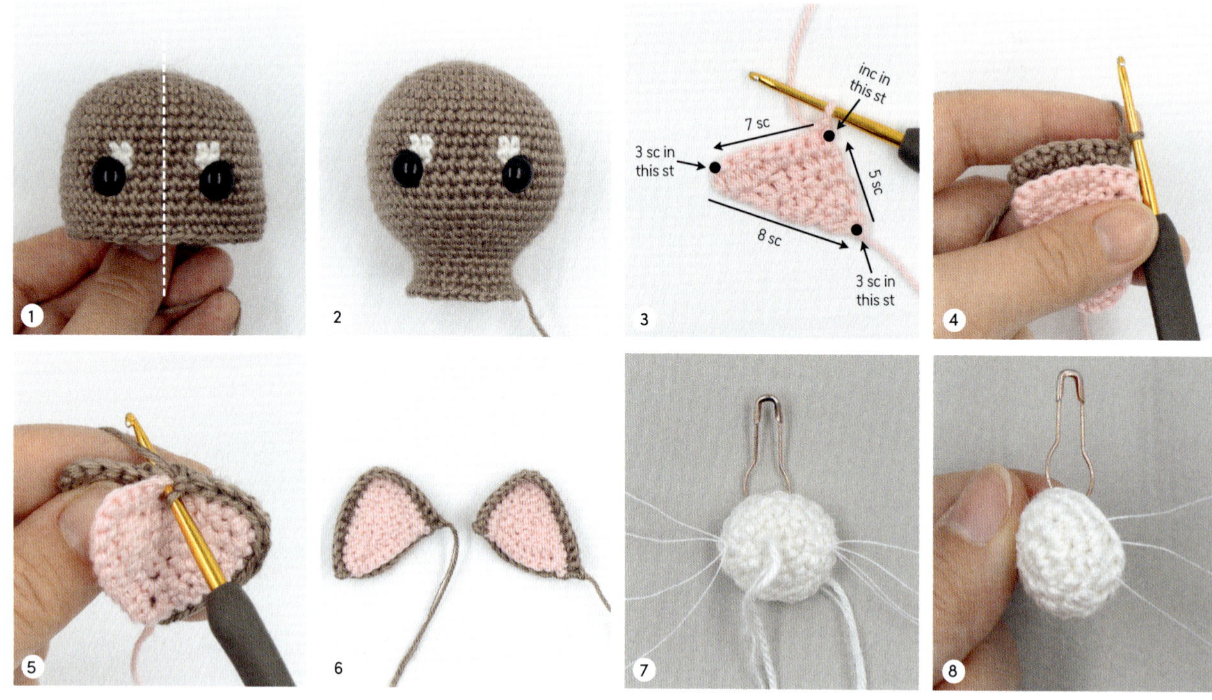

Stuff the head with fiberfill and continue stuffing as you go 1.

Rnd 20: (sc in next 5 st, dec) repeat 6 times [36]
Rnd 21: (sc in next 2 st, dec, sc in next 2 st) repeat 6 times [30]
Rnd 22: (sc in next 3 st, dec) repeat 6 times [24]
Rnd 23 – 24: sc in all 24 st [24]
Rnd 25: (sc in next 7 st, inc in next st) repeat 3 times [27]
Rnd 26: (sc in next 4 st, inc in next st, sc in next 4 st) repeat 3 times [30]
Rnd 27: (sc in next 9 st, inc in next st) repeat 3 times [33]
Fasten off, leaving a yarn tail for sewing 2.

RIGHT EAR

Inner part (in pink yarn)

Ch 2. Crochet in rows.
Row 1: start in second ch from hook, inc in this ch, ch 1, turn [2]
Row 2: sc in next st, inc in next st, ch 1, turn [3]
Row 3: sc in next 2 st, inc in next st, ch 2, turn [4]
Row 4: dc inc in next st, hdc in next st, sc in next 2 st, ch 1, turn [5]
Row 5: sc in next 2 st, hdc in next st, dc in next st, dc inc in next st, ch 2, turn [6]
Row 6: dc inc in next st, dc in next st, hdc inc in next st, sc in next 3 st [8]
Next, we crochet around the ear 3.
Row 7: ch 1, turn, sc in next 7 st, 3 sc in next st, continue in the row-ends on the longer side of the ear, sc in next 8 st, 3 sc in next st, continue in the row-ends on the shorter side of the ear, sc in next 5 st, inc in next st [28]
Fasten off and set aside.

Outer part (in brown yarn)

Ch 2. Crochet in rows.
Row 1 – 7: repeat the instructions for the inner part, but don't fasten off.

In the next row, we'll join the inner and outer parts together.
Row 8: ch 1, turn, place the inner part on top of your work with the wrong side facing up and crochet through both layers 4 5, sc in next 20 st, ch 1, turn [20] Leave the remaining stitches unworked.
Row 9: sc in all 20 st [20]
Fasten off, leaving a brown yarn tail for sewing. Weave in all other yarn ends.

LEFT EAR

Inner part (in pink yarn)

Ch 2. Crochet in rows.
Row 1: start in second ch from hook, inc in this ch, ch 1, turn [2]
Row 2: sc in next st, inc in next st, ch 1, turn [3]
Row 3: sc in next 2 st, inc in next st, ch 1, turn [4]
Row 4: sc in next 2 st, hdc in next st, dc inc in next st, ch 2, turn [5]
Row 5: dc inc in next st, dc in next st, hdc in next st, sc in next 2 st, ch 1, turn [6]
Row 6: sc in next 3 st, hdc inc in next st, dc in next st, dc inc in next st [8]
Next, we crochet around the ear.
Row 7: ch 1, turn, sc in next 7 st, 3 sc in next st, continue in the row-ends on the shorter side of the ear, sc in next 5 st, 3 sc in next st, continue in the row-ends on the longer side of the ear, sc in next 8 st, inc in next st [28]
Fasten off and set aside.

Outer part (in brown yarn)

Ch 2. Crochet in rows.
Row 1 – 7: repeat the instructions for the inner part, but don't fasten off. In the next row, we'll join the inner and outer parts together.
Row 8: ch 1, turn, place the inner part on top of your work with the wrong side facing up and crochet through both layers, sc in next 20 st, ch 1, turn [20] Leave the remaining stitches unworked.
Row 9: sc in all 20 st [20]
Fasten off, leaving a brown yarn tail for sewing. Weave in all other yarn ends 6.

SNOUT (in white yarn)

Rnd 1: start 7 sc in a magic ring [7]
Rnd 2: inc in all 7 st [14]
Rnd 3: sc in next 10 st, hdc inc in next st, dc in next 3 st [15]
Rnd 4: dc in next 2 st, hdc inc in next st, sc in next 4 st *(mark the last sc with a stitch marker),* sc in next 5 st [13] Leave the remaining stitches unworked.
Fasten off, leaving a yarn tail for sewing.

Attach the whiskers

Prepare 4 strands of white sewing thread, each about 6" / 15 cm long. Note that the marked stitch indicates the top center of the snout. With the wrong side of the snout facing you, tie 2 strands on the left and 2 strands on the right, keeping the knots on the inside so they remain hidden from the front 7 Each knot creates 2 loose ends, giving you 4 strands on each side. Pull each strand through a separate stitch gap to the front side of the snout 8.

BODY

Sweater (in teal yarn)

Rnd 1: start 6 sc in a magic ring [6]
Rnd 2: inc in all 6 st [12]
Rnd 3: (sc in next st, inc in next st) repeat 6 times [18]
Rnd 4: (sc in next st, inc in next st, sc in next st) repeat 6 times [24]
Rnd 5: (sc in next 3 st, inc in next st) repeat 6 times [30]
Rnd 6: (sc in next 2 st, inc in next st, sc in next 2 st) repeat 6 times [36]
Rnd 7: (sc in next 5 st, inc in next st) repeat 6 times [42]
Rnd 8 – 13: sc in all 42 st [42]
Rnd 14: (sc in next 6 st, dec, sc in next 6 st) repeat 3 times [39]
Rnd 15: (sc in next 11 st, dec) repeat 3 times [36]
Rnd 16 – 18: sc in all 36 st [36]
Rnd 19: (sc in next 11 st, inc in next st) repeat 3 times [39]
Rnd 20: (sc in next 6 st, inc in next st, sc in next 6 st) repeat 3 times [42]

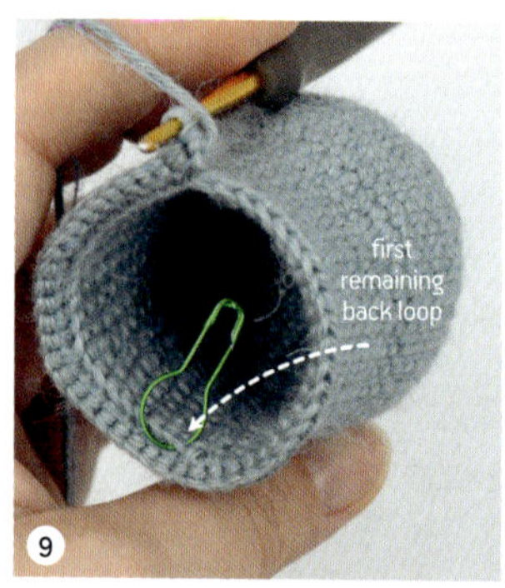

9

10

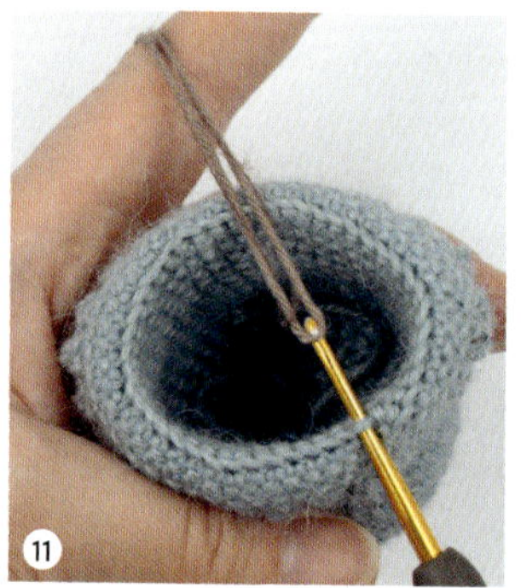
11

12

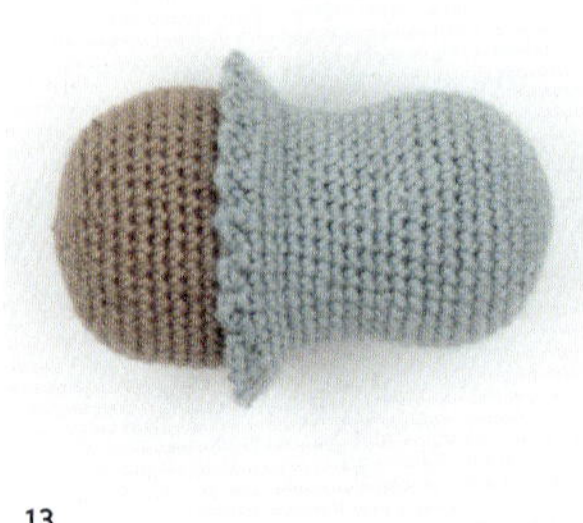
13

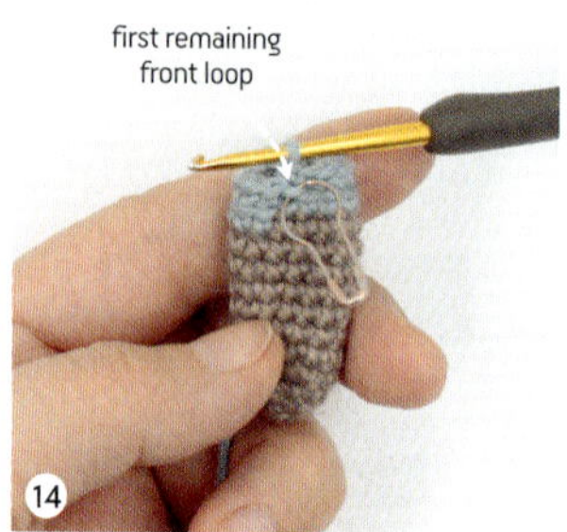

14

15

16

Rnd 21: (sc in next 13 st, inc in next st) repeat 3 times [45]
Work the next round in FLO *(and mark the first remaining back loop with a stitch marker 9).*
Rnd 22: FLO (sc in next 7 st, inc in next st, sc in next 7 st) repeat 3 times [48]
Rnd 23: sc in all 48 st [48]
Rnd 24: sc in next st, (ch 5, sc in next 2 st) repeat 23 times, ch 5, sc in next st [48 + 24 ch-spaces] 10
Fasten off and weave in the yarn end.

Lower body (in brown yarn)
Pull up a loop of brown yarn in the marked first leftover back loop of the sweater. Fold the hem of the sweater outward to make it easier to access the remaining back loops 11. Work the first stitch in the same stitch where you attached the yarn.
Rnd 1: work this round in BLO, ch 1, (sc in next 7 st, inc in next st, sc in next 7 st) repeat 3 times [48] 12
Stuff the body with fiberfill and continue stuffing as you go.
Rnd 2 – 11: sc in all 48 st [48]
Rnd 12: (sc in next 3 st, dec, sc in next 3 st) repeat 6 times [42]
Rnd 13: (sc in next 5 st, dec) repeat 6 times [36]
Rnd 14: (sc in next 2 st, dec, sc in next 2 st) repeat 6 times [30]
Rnd 15: (sc in next 3 st, dec) repeat 6 times [24]
Rnd 16: (sc in next st, dec, sc in next st) repeat 6 times [18]
Rnd 17: (sc in next st, dec) repeat 6 times [12]
Rnd 18: dec 6 times [6]
Fasten off, leaving a yarn tail. Using a yarn needle, weave the yarn tail through the front loop of each remaining stitch and pull it tight to close. Weave in the yarn ends 13.

FRONT LEG (make 2)

Main part (start in brown yarn)
Rnd 1: start 6 sc in a magic ring [6]
Rnd 2: (sc in next st, inc in next st) repeat 3 times [9]
Rnd 3: (sc in next st, inc in next st, sc in next st) repeat 3 times [12]
Rnd 4: sc in all 12 st [12]

Rnd 5: sc in next 11 st, inc in next st [13]
Rnd 6: sc in all 13 st [13]
Rnd 7: sc in next 6 st, inc in next st, sc in next 6 st [14]
Rnd 8 – 10: sc in all 14 st [14]
Change to teal yarn.
Rnd 11: sc in all 14 st [14]
Work the next round in BLO *(and mark the first remaining front loop with a stitch marker).*
Rnd 12: BLO sc in all 14 st [14] (14)
Rnd 13: sc in next 13 st, inc in next st [15]
Rnd 14: sc in next 7 st, inc in next st, sc in next 5 st, ch 1, turn [14] Leave the remaining stitches unworked.
Continue crocheting in rows.
Row 15: skip first sc, sc in next 10 st, ch 1, turn [10] Leave the remaining stitches unworked (15).
Row 16: skip first sc, sc in next 9 st, ch 1, turn [9]
Row 17: skip first sc, sc in next 8 st, ch 1, turn [8]
Row 18: skip first sc, sc in next st, hdc in next st, dc in next 3 st, hdc in next st, sc in next st [7]
Fasten off, leaving a yarn tail for sewing.

Sleeve (in teal yarn)
Hold the leg upside down and pull up a loop of teal yarn in the marked first leftover front loop of the leg (16).
Rnd 1: work this round in FLO, ch 1, sc in the same stitch where you attached the yarn, (sc in next 2 st, inc in next st) repeat 2 times, sc in next 3 st, inc in next st, sc in next 2 st, inc in next st [18] (17)
Rnd 2: sc in next st, (ch 4, sc in next 2 st) repeat 8 times, ch 4, slst in next st [18 + 9 ch-spaces]
Fasten off and weave in the yarn ends. Stuff the leg with fiberfill (18).

HIND LEG (make 2)

Foot (in brown yarn)
Rnd 1: start 6 sc in a magic ring [6]
Rnd 2: inc in all 6 st [12]
Rnd 3 – 5: sc in all 12 st [12]
Rnd 6: sc in all 12 st, ch 1, turn [12]

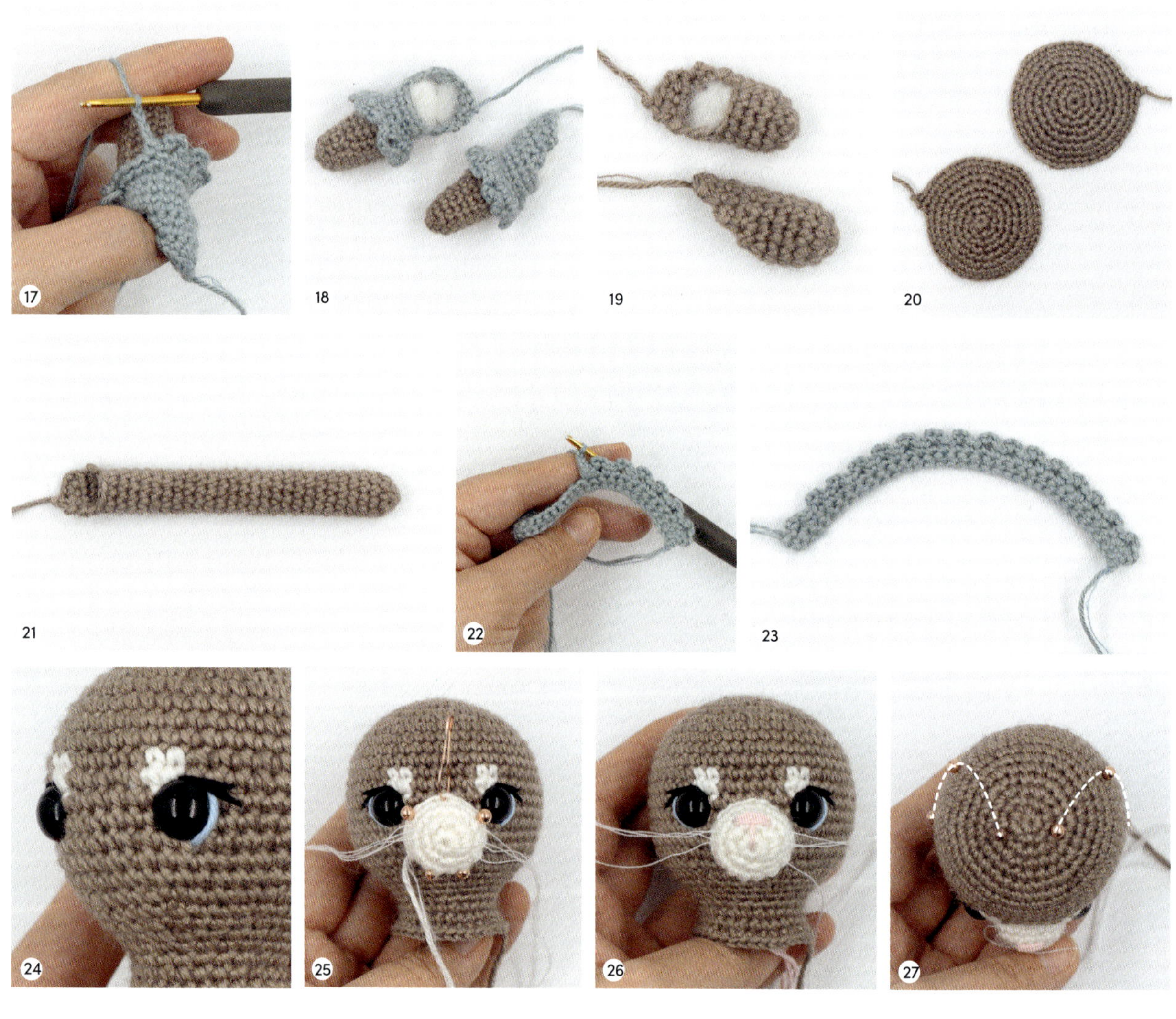
17 18 19 20 21 22 23 24 25 26 27

Continue crocheting in rows.

Row 7: skip first sc, sc in next 7 st, ch 1, turn [7] Leave the remaining stitches unworked.

Row 8: skip first sc, sc in next 6 st, ch 1, turn [6]

Row 9: skip first sc, sc in next 5 st, ch 1, turn [5]

Row 10: skip first sc, sc in next 4 st, ch 1, turn [4]

Row 11: skip first sc, sc in next 3 st [3]

Fasten off, leaving a yarn tail for sewing. Stuff with fiberfill 19.

Upper part (in brown yarn)

Rnd 1: start 6 sc in a magic ring [6]

Rnd 2: inc in all 6 st [12]

Rnd 3: (sc in next st, inc in next st) repeat 6 times [18]

Rnd 4: (sc in next st, inc in next st, sc in next st) repeat 6 times [24]

Rnd 5: (sc in next 3 st, inc in next st) repeat 6 times [30]

Rnd 6: (sc in next 2 st, inc in next st, sc in next 2 st) repeat 6 times [36]

Rnd 7: (sc in next 5 st, inc in next st) repeat 6 times [42]
Rnd 8: (sc in next 13 st, inc in next st) repeat 3 times [45]
Fasten off, leaving a yarn tail for sewing 20.

TAIL (in brown yarn)
Rnd 1: start 5 sc in a magic ring [5]
Rnd 2: inc in all 5 st [10]
Rnd 3 – 27: sc in all 10 st [10]
Rnd 28: sc in all 10 st, ch 1, turn [10]
Continue crocheting in rows.
Row 29: skip first sc, sc in next 5 st, ch 1, turn [5] Leave the remaining stitches unworked.
Row 30: skip first sc, sc in next 4 st, ch 1, turn [4]
Row 31: skip first sc, sc in next 3 st [3]
Fasten off, leaving a yarn tail for sewing 21.

TURTLENECK (in teal yarn)
Ch 34. Crochet in rows
Row 1: start in second ch from hook, sc in next 33 ch, ch 1, turn [33]
Row 2: sc in next st, (ch 3, sc in next 2 st) repeat 16 times [33 + 16 ch-spaces] 22 23
Fasten off, leaving a long yarn tail for sewing.

ASSEMBLY

Make the eyes colorful

- Using several strands of blue thread, embroider a line along the outer edge of each eye.
- Using black thread, embroider the upper outline and eye-lashes 24.

Attach the snout

- Position the snout just below the eyes, with the stitch marker centered between them 25. Pin the snout in place, remove the stitch marker and sew around using the remaining yarn tail.
- Using pink thread, embroider a nose between rounds 2-3 on the top side of the snout. Then, add a short vertical line below the nose to create a T-shape. 26.

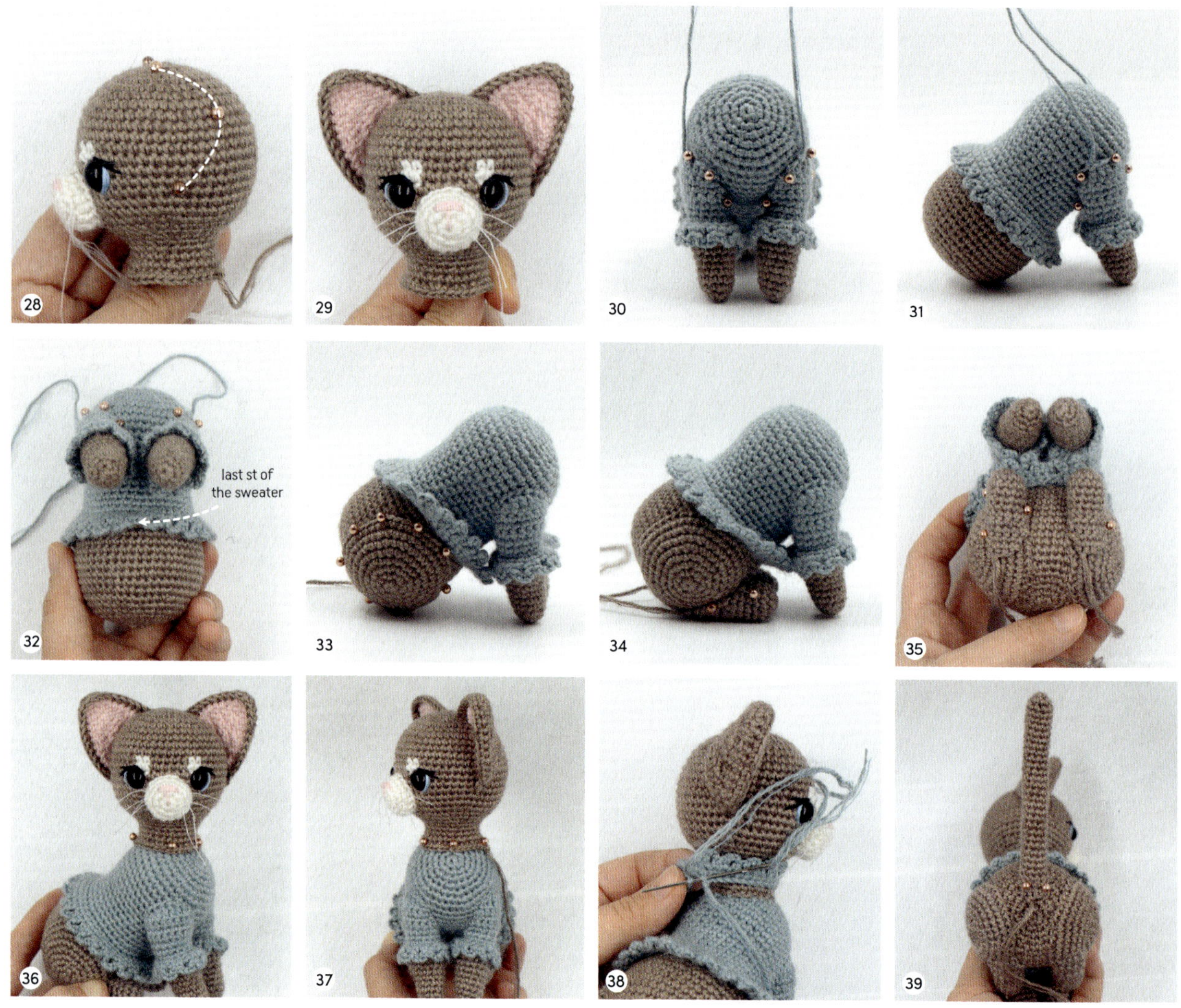

• Cut the whiskers to the desired length. You get the cutest look when each whisker is a slightly different length.

Attach the ears

• Position the ears on both sides of the head, between rounds 3-14 27 28. Pin them in place and sew them on using the remaining yarn tails 29.

Attach the front legs

• Place the front legs on the teal side of the body, covering rounds 8-15 of the sweater 30 31. The longer edges of the legs should face outward. Ensure the last stitch of the sweater hem is centered on the cat's belly to keep it hidden 32. Pin them in place and sew around using the remaining yarn tails.

Attach the hind legs

• Place the upper parts of the hind legs on the lower sides of the body. It's easiest to do this while your cat is sitting on a flat surface. The top should be positioned on round 1 of the lower body, right below the sweater hem. Pin them in place and sew around using the remaining yarn tails. Add more stuffing before closing the seam 33.

- Pin the feet below the upper parts of the hind legs. The feet should be facing the front side of the cat. Sew around using the remaining yarn tails 34 35.

Attach the head

- Place the head on top of the body, it should cover rounds 2-10 of the sweater. Turn the head to the side to give your cat a cuter look. Pin it in place and sew around using the remaining yarn tail 36 37.

Attach the turtleneck

- Wrap the turtleneck around the neck and sew the ends together using the remaining yarn tail 38, but don't weave in the end yet.
- Pin the turtleneck to the body and sew it to the body using the same yarn tail.

Attach the tail

- If you want the tail to be posable, insert the wire or pipe cleaner. Otherwise, lightly stuff it with fiberfill.
- Position the tail on the back of the body, with the tail pointing upward. Pin it in place and sew around using the remaining yarn tail 39.
- If you've inserted a wire, you can shape the tail to your liking.

DAISY
the Chihuahua

Skill level: 
Size: 5" / 12.5 cm tall (standing) or 4.3" / 11 cm tall (seated) when made with the indicated yarn.

Amigurumi gallery: Scan or visit www.amigurumi.com/5504 to share pictures and find inspiration.

MATERIALS

• Sport weight yarn in cream, beige, green, light green and pink • B-1 / 2.25 mm crochet hook • Safety eyes (12 mm) • Black and white embroidery thread • Yarn needle • Pins • Stitch markers • Fiberfill for stuffing • 4 pieces of wire or pipe cleaner of approx. 2" / 5 cm (for the legs) • Optional: super fine weight mohair yarn in cream, beige, green, light green and pink *(if you decide to crochet using two strands of yarn)*

NOTE

To achieve the soft texture shown in the photos, I crocheted with two strands held together: one strand of sport weight cotton and one strand of super fine weight mohair in a matching color. This is completely optional, using a single strand of yarn works just as well.

Follow the main instructions to make a standing Chihuahua. If you would like to make the sitting dog instead, be sure to read the additional instructions on page 45 first.

HEAD (in cream yarn)
Rnd 1: start 6 sc in a magic ring [6]
Rnd 2: inc in all 6 st [12]
Rnd 3: (sc in next st, inc in next st) repeat 6 times [18]
Rnd 4: (sc in next st, inc in next st, sc in next st) repeat 6 times [24]
Rnd 5: (sc in next 3 st, inc in next st) repeat 6 times [30]
Rnd 6: (sc in next 2 st, inc in next st, sc in next 2 st) repeat 6 times [36]
Rnd 7: (sc in next 5 st, inc in next st) repeat 6 times [42]
Rnd 8: (sc in next 3 st, inc in next st, sc in next 3 st) repeat 6 times [48]
Rnd 9 – 16: sc in all 48 st [48]
Rnd 17: (sc in next 3 st, dec, sc in next 3 st) repeat 6 times [42]
Insert the safety eyes between rounds 13 and 14, with an interspace of 9 stitches.
Stuff the head with fiberfill and continue stuffing as you go.
Rnd 18: (sc in next 5 st, dec) repeat 6 times [36]
Rnd 19: (sc in next 2 st, dec, sc in next 2 st) repeat 6 times [30]
Rnd 20: (sc in next 3 st, dec) repeat 6 times [24]

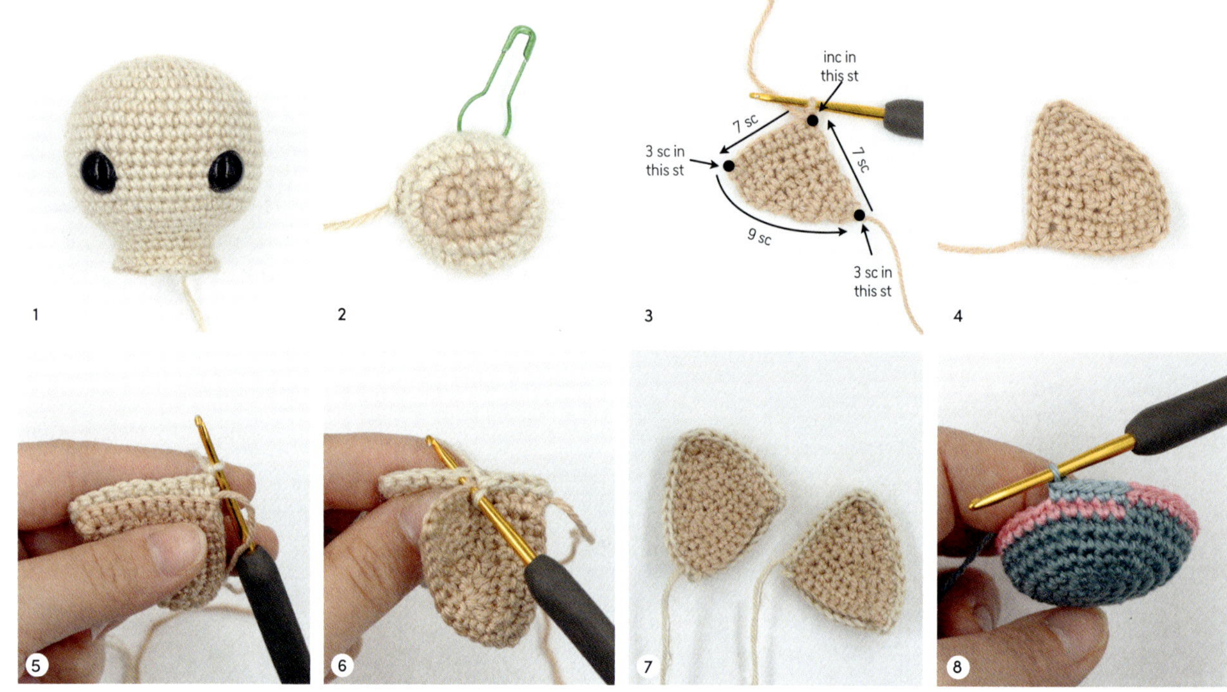

Rnd 21 – 23: sc in all 24 st [24]
Rnd 24: (sc in next 3 st, inc in next st) repeat 6 times [30]
Fasten off, leaving a yarn tail for sewing (1).

EYELID (make 2, in cream yarn)
Crochet 4 ch and fasten off, leaving a yarn tail for sewing.

SNOUT (start in beige yarn)
Leave a starting yarn tail. Ch 4. Stitches are worked around both sides of the foundation chain.
Rnd 1: start in second ch from hook, inc in this ch, sc in next ch, 4 sc in last ch. Continue on the other side of the foundation chain, sc in next ch, inc in next ch [10]
Rnd 2: inc in next 2 st, sc in next st, inc in next 2 st, change to cream yarn, inc in next 2 st, sc in next st, inc in next 2 st [18]
Rnd 3: sc in all 18 st [18]
Using a yarn needle, weave the starting yarn tail through the foundation chain to hide the stitch gaps.
Rnd 4: sc in next 2 st, hdc inc in next st, dc in next 4 st, hdc inc in next st, sc in next 7 st *(mark the last sc with a stitch marker)*, sc in next 3 st [20]
Rnd 5: sc in next 2 st [2] Leave the remaining stitches unworked. Fasten off, leaving a yarn tail for sewing. Stuff the snout with fiberfill (2).

RIGHT EAR

Inner part (in beige yarn)
Ch 2. Crochet in rows.
Row 1: start in second ch from hook, inc in this ch, ch 1, turn [2]
Row 2: sc in next st, inc in next st, ch 1, turn [3]
Row 3: sc in next 2 st, inc in next st, ch 2, turn [4]
Row 4: dc inc in next st, hdc in next st, sc in next 2 st, ch 1, turn [5]
Row 5: sc in next 2 st, hdc in next st, dc in next st, dc inc in next st, ch 2, turn [6]
Row 6: dc inc in next st, dc in next st, hdc inc in next st, sc in next 3 st, ch 1, turn [8]
Row 7 – 8: sc in all 8 st, ch 1, turn [8]

Next, we crochet around the ear 3.
Row 9: sc in next 7 st, 3 sc in next st, continue in the row-ends on the longer side of the ear, sc in next 9 st, 3 sc in next st, continue in the row-ends on the shorter side of the ear, sc in next 7 st, inc in next st [31]
Fasten off and set aside 4.

Outer part (in cream yarn)
Ch 2. Crochet in rows.
Row 1 – 9: repeat the instructions for the inner part, but don't fasten off. In the next row, we'll join the inner and outer parts together.
Row 10: ch 1, turn, place the inner part on top of your work with the wrong side facing up and crochet through both layers 5 6, sc in next 23 st [23] Leave the remaining stitches unworked.
Fasten off, leaving a cream yarn tail for sewing. Weave in all other yarn ends.

LEFT EAR

Inner part (in beige yarn)
Ch 2. Crochet in rows.
Row 1: start in second ch from hook, inc in this ch, ch 1, turn [2]
Row 2: sc in next st, inc in next st, ch 1, turn [3]
Row 3: sc in next 2 st, inc in next st, ch 1, turn [4]
Row 4: sc in next 2 st, hdc in next st, dc inc in next st, ch 2, turn [5]
Row 5: dc inc in next st, dc in next st, hdc in next st, sc in next 2 st, ch 1, turn [6]
Row 6: sc in next 3 st, hdc inc in next st, dc in next st, dc inc in next st, ch 1, turn [8]
Row 7 – 8: sc in all 8 st, ch 1, turn [8]
Next, we crochet around the ear.
Row 9: sc in next 7 st, 3 sc in next st, continue in the row-ends on the shorter side of the ear, sc in next 7 st, 3 sc in next st, continue in the row-ends on the longer side of the ear, sc in next 9 st, inc in next st [31]
Fasten off and set aside.

Outer part (in cream yarn)
Ch 2. Crochet in rows.
Row 1 – 9: repeat the instructions for the inner part, but don't fasten off. In the next row, we'll join the inner and outer parts together.
Row 10: ch 1, turn, place the inner part on top of your work with the wrong side facing up and crochet through both layers, sc in next 23 st [23] Leave the remaining stitches unworked.
Fasten off, leaving a cream yarn tail for sewing. Weave in all other yarn ends 7.

BODY

Sweater (start in green yarn)
Rnd 1: start 6 sc in a magic ring [6]
Rnd 2: inc in all 6 st [12]
Rnd 3: (sc in next st, inc in next st) repeat 6 times [18]

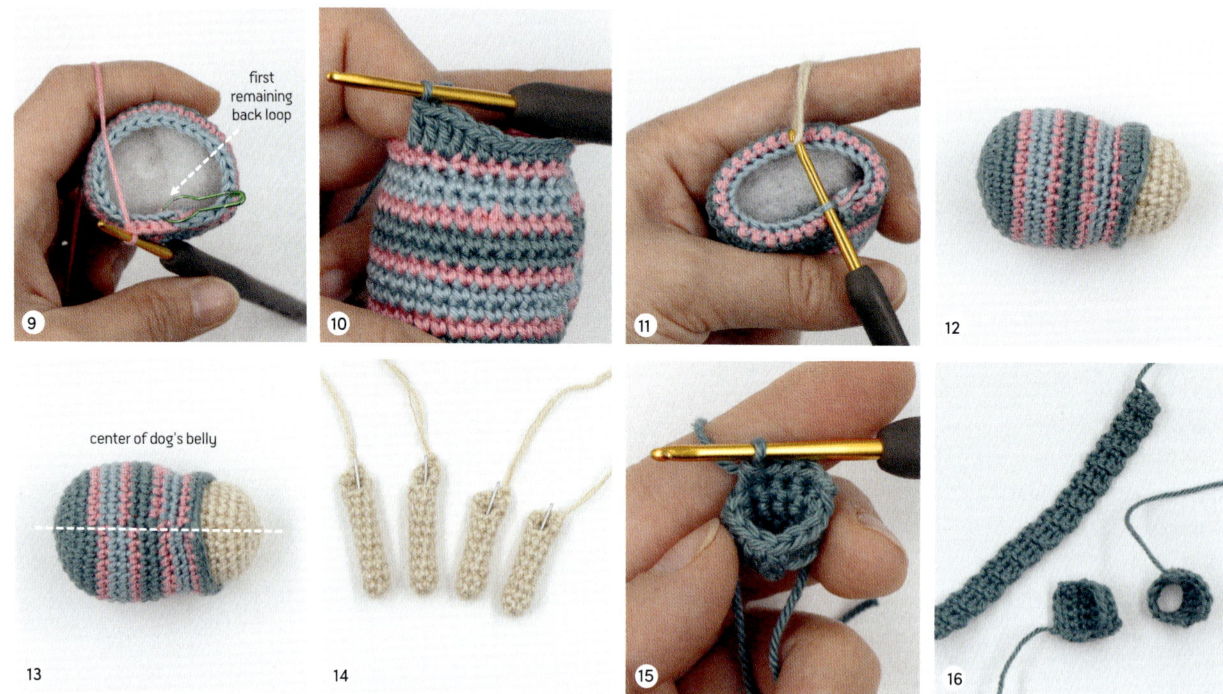

Rnd 4: (sc in next st, inc in next st, sc in next st) repeat 6 times [24]
Rnd 5: (sc in next 3 st, inc in next st) repeat 6 times [30]
Rnd 6: (sc in next 2 st, inc in next st, sc in next 2 st) repeat 6 times [36]
Rnd 7: sc in all 36 st [36]
In the next rounds, we'll alternate between pink, green and light green yarn. The color change is indicated in italics.
Rnd 8: *(pink)* sc in all 36 st [36]
Rnd 9 – 10: *(light green)* sc in all 36 st [36] (8)
Rnd 11: *(pink)* sc in all 36 st [36]
Rnd 12 – 13: *(green)* sc in all 36 st [36]
Sc in next st. This is the new start of the round.
Rnd 14: *(pink)* sc in all 36 st [36]
Rnd 15: *(light green)* (sc in next 5 st, dec, sc in next 5 st) repeat 3 times [33]
Rnd 16: *(light green)* (sc in next 9 st, dec) repeat 3 times [30]
Stuff the body with fiberfill and continue stuffing as you go. Work the next round in FLO *(and mark the first remaining back loop with a stitch marker).*
Rnd 17: *(pink)* FLO sc in all 30 st [30] (9)
Rnd 18: *(green)* sc in next 6 st, hdc in next 2 st, dc inc in next st, dc in next 12 st, dc inc in next st, hdc in next 2 st, sc in next 6 st [32] (10)
Fasten off with an invisible join. Weave in the yarn end.

Lower body (in cream yarn)
Pull up a loop of cream yarn in the marked leftover back loop of round 17 (11). Work the first stitch in the same stitch where you attached the yarn.
Rnd 1: work this round in BLO, ch 1, sc in next 4 st, skip next st, (sc in next 4 st, skip next st) repeat 5 times [24]
Rnd 2 – 6: sc in all 24 st [24]
Rnd 7: (sc in next st, dec, sc in next st) repeat 6 times [18]
Rnd 8: (sc in next st, dec) repeat 6 times [12]
Rnd 9: dec 6 times [6]
Fasten off, leaving a yarn tail. Using a yarn needle, weave the yarn tail through the front loop of each remaining stitch

and pull it tight to close. Weave in the yarn end 12 13.

TAIL (in cream yarn)
Ch 13. Crochet in rows.
Row 1: start in second ch from hook, slst in next 12 ch [12]
Fasten off, leaving a yarn tail for sewing.

FRONT LEG (make 2, in cream yarn)
Rnd 1: start 7 sc in a magic ring [7]
Rnd 2 – 9: sc in all 7 st [7]
Rnd 10: sc in all 7 st, ch 1, turn [7]
Continue crocheting in rows.
Row 11: skip first sc, sc in next 3 st, ch 1, turn [3] Leave the remaining stitches unworked.
Row 12: skip first sc, sc in next 2 st [2]
Fasten off, leaving a yarn tail for sewing. Insert the pipe cleaner or wire into the leg.

HIND LEG (make 2, in cream yarn)
Rnd 1: start 7 sc in a magic ring [7]
Rnd 2 – 7: sc in all 7 st [7]
Rnd 8: sc in all 7 st, ch 1, turn [7]
Continue crocheting in rows.
Row 9: skip first sc, sc in next 4 st, ch 1, turn [4] Leave the remaining stitches unworked.
Row 10: skip first sc, sc in next 3 st [3]
Fasten off, leaving a yarn tail for sewing. Insert the pipe cleaner or wire into the leg 14.

SLEEVE (make 2, in green yarn)
Ch 12.
Rnd 1: start in first ch to form a circle *(make sure the chains aren't twisted)*, sc in all 12 ch [12]
Rnd 2: sc in next 10 st, ch 1, turn [10] Leave the remaining stitches unworked.
Continue crocheting in rows 15.
Row 3: skip first sc, sc in next 7 st, ch 1, turn [7] Leave the remaining stitches unworked.
Row 4: skip first sc, sc in next 6 st, ch 1, turn [6]
Row 5: skip first sc, sc in next 5 st [5]

Fasten off, leaving a yarn tail for sewing.

TURTLENECK (in green yarn)
Ch 4. Crochet in rows.
Row 1: start in second ch from hook, sc in next 3 ch, ch 1, turn [3]
Row 2 – 27: BLO sc in next 3 st, ch 1, turn [3]
Row 28: BLO sc in next 3 st [3]
Fasten off, leaving a yarn tail for sewing 16.

ASSEMBLY

Attach the snout

- Position the snout just below the eyes, with the stitch marker centered between them 17. Pin the snout in place, remove the stitch marker and sew around using the remaining yarn tail.

- Using black thread, embroider a nose over rounds 2-3 of the top side of the snout 18.

Assemble the eyes

- Using several strands of white thread, embroider a line along the outer edge of each eye.
- Sew the eyelids above the safety eyes 19.

Attach the ears

- Position the ears on both sides of the head, between rounds 4-14 20 21 22. Pin them in place and sew them on using the remaining yarn tails.

Attach the legs

- Place the legs on the lower side of the body, pointing down. Keep in mind that the color changes of the body mark the center of the dog's belly. Insert the ends of the wire into the body through the stitch gaps. The front legs should be on rounds 8-10 of the sweater and the hind legs should be on rounds 5-7 of the lower body.

- Pin them in place and check to see if the dog can stand properly. Adjust the position if needed and sew around using the remaining yarn tails 23 24.

Attach the tail

- Pin the tail on the upper side of the body, on round 25, and sew around using the remaining yarn tail 25.

Attach the sleeves

- Pin the sleeves on the dog's front legs. The longer sides of the sleeves (worked in rows) should face outward. Sew around using the remaining yarn tail 26.

Attach the head

- Place the head on top of the body. It should cover rounds 4-13 of the sweater. Turn the head slightly to the side to give the dog a cuter look. Pin the head in place and sew around using the remaining yarn tail 27.

Attach the turtleneck

- Wrap the turtleneck around the neck and sew the ends together using the remaining yarn tail. Don't weave in the end yet 28.
- Pin the turtleneck to the body and sew it to the body using the same yarn tail.

How to make a seated Chihuahua

Attach the front legs

- Place the front legs on the front side of the body, covering rounds 8-10 of the sweater. Keep in mind that the color changes of the body mark the center of the dog's belly. Insert the ends of the wire into the body through the stitch gaps.
- Pin them in place and check to see if the dog can sit properly. Adjust the position if needed and sew around using the remaining yarn tails.

Attach the hind legs

- Place the hind legs on the back sides of the body, they should point to the front. It's easiest to do this while your dog is sitting on a flat surface. The hind legs should be on rounds 5-7 of the body, with an interspace of 7 stitches between them.
- Insert the ends of the wire into the body through the stitch gaps.
- Pin the legs in place and sew around using the remaining yarn tails.

Attach the head on top of the body

- Ignore the indicated rounds in the instructions, but instead aim for the head to be placed vertically.

BART
the Corgi

Skill level: ●●○
Size: 4.7" / 12 cm tall when made with the indicated yarn.

Amigurumi gallery: Scan or visit www.amigurumi.com/5505 to share pictures and find inspiration.

MATERIALS

• Sport weight yarn in orange, amber and white • B-1 / 2.25 mm crochet hook • Safety eyes (8 mm) • Black and white embroidery thread • Yarn needle • Pins • Stitch markers • Fiberfill for stuffing • Optional: White sewing thread *(for the assembly tip)*

HEAD (in orange yarn)

Rnd 1: start 6 sc in a magic ring [6]
Rnd 2: inc in all 6 st [12]
Rnd 3: (sc in next st, inc in next st) repeat 6 times [18]
Rnd 4: (sc in next st, inc in next st, sc in next st) repeat 6 times [24]
Rnd 5: (sc in next 3 st, inc in next st) repeat 6 times [30]
Rnd 6: (sc in next 2 st, inc in next st, sc in next 2 st) repeat 6 times [36]
Rnd 7: (sc in next 5 st, inc in next st) repeat 6 times [42]
Rnd 8: (sc in next 3 st, inc in next st, sc in next 3 st) repeat 6 times [48]
Rnd 9 – 16: sc in all 48 st [48]
Rnd 17: (sc in next 3 st, dec, sc in next 3 st) repeat 6 times [42]
Rnd 18: (sc in next 5 st, dec) repeat 6 times [36]
Insert the safety eyes between rounds 13 and 14, with an interspace of 8 stitches. Stuff the head with fiberfill and continue stuffing as you go.
Rnd 19: (sc in next 2 st, dec, sc in next 2 st) repeat 6 times [30]
Rnd 20: (sc in next 3 st, dec) repeat 6 times [24]
Rnd 21 – 22: sc in all 24 st [24]
Rnd 23: (sc in next 3 st, inc in next st) repeat 6 times [30]
Fasten off, leaving a yarn tail for sewing (1).

BODY (in orange yarn)

Rnd 1: start 6 sc in a magic ring [6]
Rnd 2: inc in all 6 st [12]
Rnd 3: (sc in next st, inc in next st) repeat 6 times [18]
Rnd 4: (sc in next st, inc in next st, sc in next st) repeat 6 times [24]
Rnd 5: (sc in next 3 st, inc in next st) repeat 6 times [30]
Rnd 6: (sc in next 2 st, inc in next st, sc in next 2 st) repeat

6 times [36]
Rnd 7 – 13: sc in all 36 st [36]
Rnd 14: (sc in next 2 st, dec, sc in next 2 st) repeat 6 times [30]
Rnd 15 – 16: sc in all 30 st [30]
Rnd 17: (sc in next 9 st, inc in next st) repeat 3 times [33]
Rnd 18: (sc in next 5 st, inc in next st, sc in next 5 st) repeat 3 times [36]
Rnd 19: (sc in next 5 st, inc in next st) repeat 6 times [42]
Rnd 20 – 25: sc in all 42 st [42]
Stuff the body with fiberfill and continue stuffing as you go.
Rnd 26: (sc in next 5 st, dec) repeat 6 times [36]
Rnd 27: (sc in next 2 st, dec, sc in next 2 st) repeat 6 times [30]
Rnd 28: (sc in next 3 st, dec) repeat 6 times [24]
Rnd 29: (sc in next st, dec, sc in next st) repeat 6 times [18]
Rnd 30: (sc in next st, dec) repeat 6 times [12]
Rnd 31: dec 6 times [6]
Fasten off, leaving a yarn tail. Using a yarn needle, weave the yarn tail through the front loop of each remaining stitch and pull it tight to close. Weave in the yarn end.

FRONT LEG (make 2, start in white yarn)
Rnd 1: start 6 sc in a magic ring [6]
Rnd 2: inc in all 6 st [12]
Rnd 3 – 5: sc in all 12 st [12]
Change to orange yarn.
Rnd 6: sc in all 12 st [12]
Rnd 7: sc in next 10 st, ch 1, turn [10] Leave the remaining stitches unworked.
Continue crocheting in rows.
Row 8: sc in next 8 st, ch 1, turn [8] Leave the remaining stitches unworked.
Row 9: skip first sc, sc in next 7 st, ch 1, turn [7]
Row 10: skip first sc, sc in next 6 st, ch 1, turn [6]
Row 11: skip first sc, sc in next 5 st , ch 1, turn [5]
Row 12: skip first sc, sc in next 4 st, ch 1, turn [4]
Row 13: skip first sc, sc in next 3 st [3]
Fasten off, leaving a yarn tail for sewing. Stuff the front legs with fiberfill (2).

HIND LEG (make 2)

Upper part (in orange yarn)
Rnd 1: start 6 sc in a magic ring [6]
Rnd 2: inc in all 6 st [12]
Rnd 3: (sc in next st, inc in next st) repeat 6 times [18]
Rnd 4: (sc in next st, inc in next st, sc in next st) repeat 6 times [24]
Rnd 5: (sc in next 3 st, inc in next st) repeat 6 times [30]
Rnd 6: (sc in next 9 st, inc in next st) repeat 3 times [33]
Fasten off, leaving a yarn tail for sewing (3).

Foot (in white yarn)
Rnd 1: start 6 sc in a magic ring [6]
Rnd 2: inc in all 6 st [12]
Rnd 3: sc in all 12 st [12]
Rnd 4: sc in all 12 st, ch 1, turn [12]
Continue crocheting in rows.

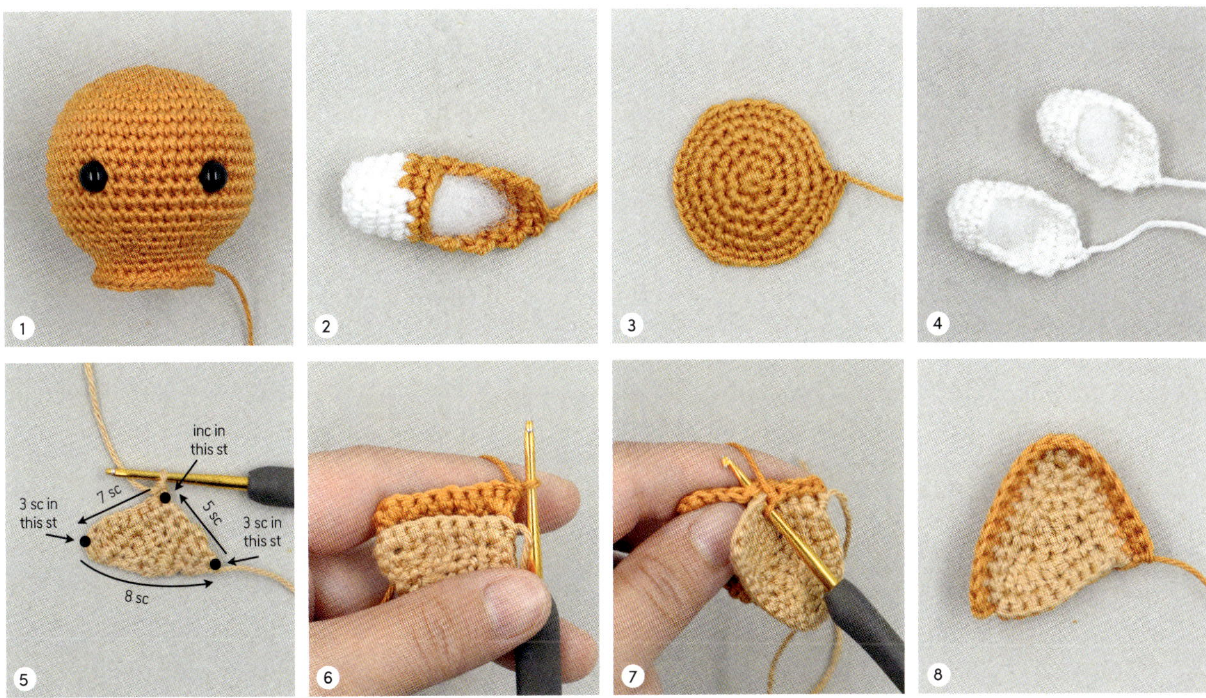

Row 5: sc in next 9 st, ch 1, turn [9] Leave the remaining stitches unworked.

Row 6: skip first sc, sc in next 8 st, ch 1, turn [8]

Row 7: skip first sc, sc in next 7 st, ch 1, turn [7]

Row 8: skip first sc, sc in next 6 st, ch 1, turn [6]

Row 9: skip first sc, sc in next 5 st, ch 1, turn [5]

Row 10: skip first sc, sc in next 4 st [4]

Fasten off, leaving a yarn tail for sewing. Stuff the feet with fiberfill 4.

RIGHT EAR

Inner part (in amber yarn)

Ch 2. Crochet in rows.

Row 1: start in second ch from hook, inc in this ch, ch 1, turn [2]

Row 2: sc in next st, inc in next st, ch 1, turn [3]

Row 3: sc in next 2 st, inc in next st, ch 2, turn [4]

Row 4: dc inc in next st, hdc in next st, sc in next 2 st, ch 1, turn [5]

Row 5: sc in next 2 st, hdc in next st, dc in next st, dc inc in next st, ch 2, turn [6]

Row 6: dc inc in next st, dc in next st, hdc inc in next st, sc in next 3 st [8]

Next, we crochet around the ear 5.

Row 7: ch 1, turn, sc in next 7 st, 3 sc in next st, continue in the row-ends on the longer side of the ear, sc in next 8 st, 3 sc in next st, continue in the row-ends on the shorter side of the ear, sc in next 5 st, inc in next st [28]

Fasten off and set aside.

Outer part (in orange yarn)

Ch 2. Crochet in rows.

Row 1 – 7: repeat the instructions for the inner part, but don't fasten off.

In the next row, we'll join the inner and outer parts together.

Row 8: ch 1, turn, place the inner part on top of your work with the wrong side facing up and crochet through both layers 6 7, sc in next 20 st, ch 1, turn [20] Leave the remaining

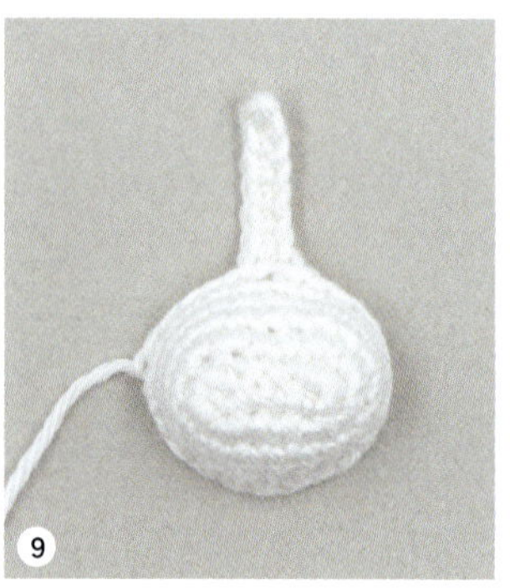
9

10

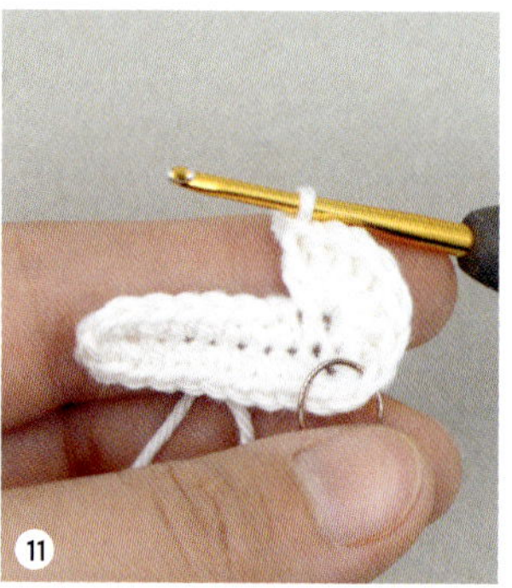
11

12

stitches unworked.

Row 9: sc in all 20 st [20]

Fasten off, leaving a long orange tail for sewing. Weave in all other yarn ends 8.

LEFT EAR

Inner part (in amber yarn)

Ch 2. Crochet in rows.

Row 1: start in second ch from hook, inc in this ch, ch 1, turn [2]

Row 2: sc in next st, inc in next st, ch 1, turn [3]

Row 3: sc in next 2 st, inc in next st, ch 1, turn [4]

Row 4: sc in next 2 st, hdc in next st, dc inc in next st, ch 2, turn [5]

Row 5: dc inc in next st, dc in next st, hdc in next st, sc in next 2 st, ch 1, turn [6]

Row 6: sc in next 3 st, hdc inc in next st, dc in next st, dc inc in next st [8]

Next, we crochet around the ear.

Row 7: ch 1, turn, sc in next 7 st, 3 sc in next st, continue in the row-ends on the shorter side of the ear, sc in next 5 st, 3 sc in next st, continue in the row-ends on the longer side of the ear, sc in next 8 st, inc in next st [28]

Fasten off and set aside.

Outer part (in orange yarn)

Ch 2. Crochet in rows.

Row 1 – 7: repeat the instructions for the inner part, but don't fasten off. In the next row, we'll join the inner and outer parts together.

Row 8: ch 1, turn, place the inner part on top of your work with the wrong side facing up and crochet through both layers, sc in next 20 st, ch 1, turn [20] Leave the remaining stitches unworked.

Row 9: sc in all 20 st [20]

Fasten off, leaving an orange yarn tail for sewing. Weave in all other yarn ends.

SNOUT (in white yarn)

Leave a starting yarn tail. Ch 5. Stitches are worked around both sides of the foundation chain.

Rnd 1: start in second ch from hook, inc in this ch, sc in next 2 ch, 4 sc in last ch. Continue on the other side of the foundation chain, sc in next 2 ch, inc in last ch [12]

Rnd 2: inc in next 2 st, sc in next 2 st, inc in next 4 st, sc in next 2 st, inc in next 2 st [20]

Rnd 3 – 4: sc in all 20 st [20]

Using a yarn needle, weave the starting yarn tail through the foundation chain to hide the stitch gaps.

In the next round, we'll make the stripe that covers the puppy's forehead.

Rnd 5: sc in next 2 st, hdc inc in next st, dc in next 5 st, hdc inc in next st, sc in next 7 st, ch 8, start in second ch from hook, sc in next 7 ch, continue on the snout, sc in next 4 st [29]

Rnd 6: sc in next 2 st [2] Leave the remaining stitches unworked.

Fasten off, leaving a yarn tail for sewing 9.

CHEST PATCH (in white yarn)

Leave a starting yarn tail. Ch 8. Stitches are worked around both sides of the foundation chain.

Rnd 1: start in second ch from hook, inc in this ch, sc in next 2 ch, hdc in next 2 ch, dc in next ch, 6 dc in last ch. Continue on the other side of the foundation chain, dc in next ch, hdc in next 2 ch, sc in next 2 ch, inc in last ch [20]

Rnd 2: slst in next 3 st, sc in next 3 st, hdc in next st, (hdc in next st, hdc inc in next st) repeat 3 times, hdc in next st, sc in next 3 st, slst in next 3 st [23]

Fasten off with an invisible join, leaving a long tail for sewing ⑩. Using a yarn needle, weave the starting yarn tail through the foundation chain to hide the stitch gaps.

BUTT PATCH (in white yarn)

Leave a starting yarn tail. Ch 10. Stitches are worked around both sides of the foundation chain.

Rnd 1: start in second ch from hook, inc in this ch, sc in next 7 ch, 4 sc in last ch. Continue on the other side of the foundation chain, sc in next 7 ch, inc in last ch [22]

Rnd 2: sc in next st, skip next st, 6 dc in next st ⑪, skip next 2 st, slst in next st, skip next 2 st, 6 dc in next st, skip next st, sc in next 3 st, hdc in next 2 st, dc in next st, 2 dc + ch 1 + 2 dc in next st, dc in next st, hdc in next 2 st, sc in next 2 st [29 + 1 ch]

Fasten off with an invisible join, leaving a long tail for sewing ⑫. Using a yarn needle, weave the starting yarn tail through the foundation chain to hide the stitch gaps.

TAIL (in orange yarn)

Rnd 1: start 6 sc in a magic ring [6]

Rnd 2: (sc in next st, inc in next st) repeat 3 times [9]

Rnd 3: sc in all 9 st [9]

Fasten off, leaving a long tail for sewing.

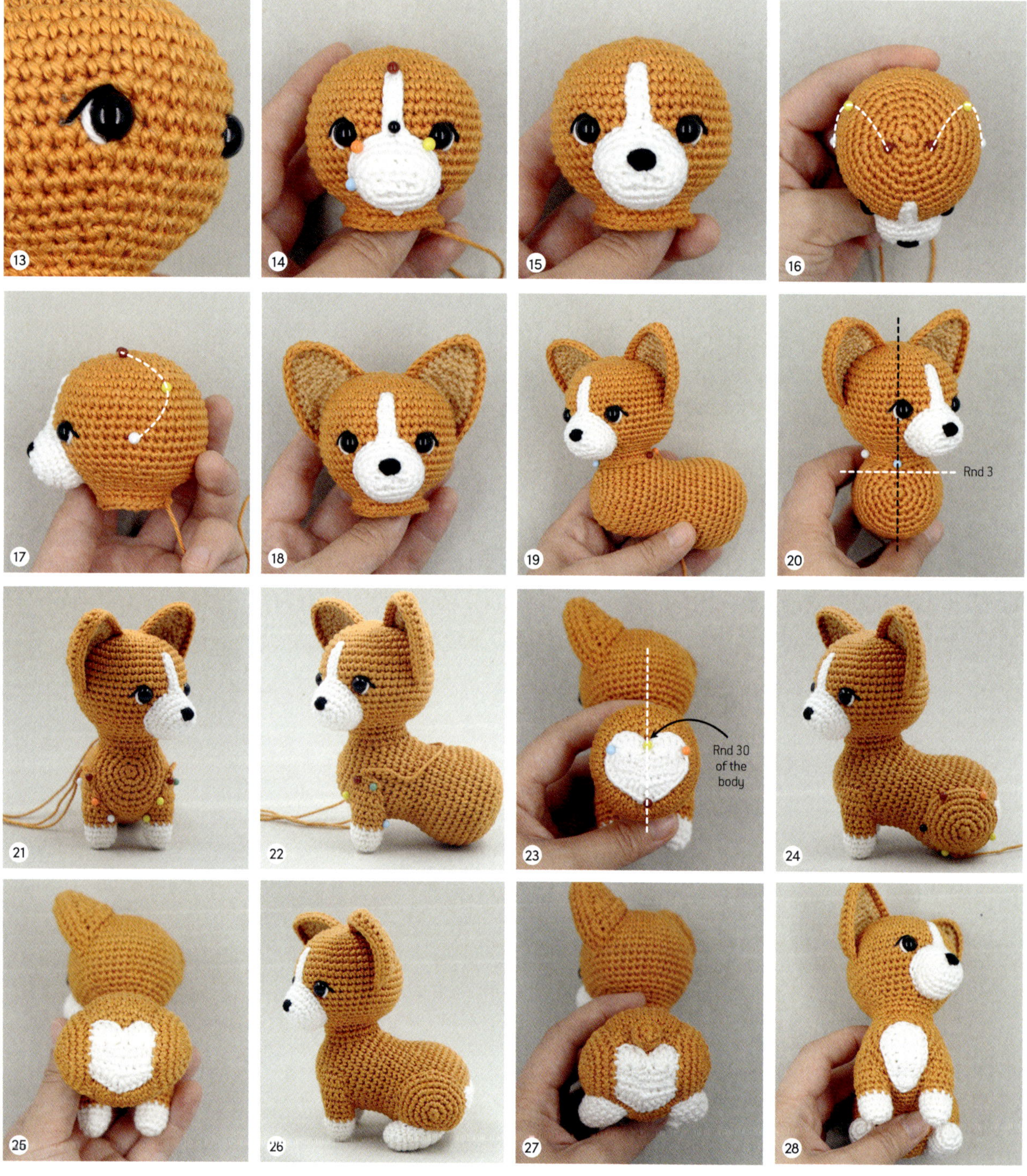
13
14
15
16
17
18
19
20
Rnd 3
21
22
23
Rnd 30 of the body
24
25
26
27
28

ASSEMBLY

TIP: Sewing white pieces onto the orange parts can be challenging. To make the seams less noticeable, try using white sewing thread and a thin needle instead of the yarn tails.

Assemble the eyes

- Using several strands of white thread, embroider a line along the outer edge of each eye.
- Using black thread, embroider the upper outline 13.

Attach the snout

- Pin the snout in place just below the safety eyes, aligning the stripe with the center of the forehead. Sew it on using the remaining yarn tail. Stuff the snout with fiberfill before closing the seam 14.

Embroider the nose

- Using a strand of black thread, embroider the nose on the top side of the snout, on round 3, aligned with the forehead stripe 15.

Attach the ears

- Position the ears on both sides of the head, between rounds 3-14 16 17. Pin them in place and sew them on using the remaining yarn tails 18.

Attach the head to the body

- Place the head on the body. Position the front neck seam on round 3 of the body and the back neck seam on round 12 19 20. The head should be slightly turned to the left. Pin it in place and sew around using the remaining yarn tail.

Attach the front legs

- Pin the front legs on the front side of the body, covering rounds 6-12. Check to see if the puppy can sit properly. Adjust the position if needed and sew around using the remaining yarn tails 21 22.

Attach the butt patch

- Place the butt patch on the back side of the body. The center of the patch should cover the last round of the body 23. Pin it in place and sew around using the remaining yarn tail.

Attach the hind legs

- Place the upper parts of the hind legs on the lower sides of the body. It's easiest to do this while your dog is sitting on a flat surface. The upper parts should cover rounds 18-27 of the body. Pin them in place and sew around using the remaining yarn tails. Add some stuffing before closing the seam 24 25.
- Place the feet below the upper parts of the hind legs. The feet should be facing the front side of the dog. Pin them in place and sew around using the remaining yarn tails 26.

Attach the tail

- Pin the tail above the butt patch and sew around using the remaining yarn tail 27.

Attach the chest patch

- Place the chest patch on the front side of the body. The wide end of the patch should cover the starting round of the body and the narrow end should be facing the belly. Pin it in place and sew around using the remaining yarn tail 28.

BARNEY
the Dachshund

Skill level: ● ● ●
Size: 5" / 12.5 cm tall, 8.3" / 21 cm long when made with the indicated yarn.

Amigurumi gallery: Scan or visit www.amigurumi.com/5506 to share pictures and find inspiration.

MATERIALS

• Sport weight yarn in brown, beige, orange and rust • B-1 / 2.25 mm crochet hook • Safety eyes (10 mm) • Black and white embroidery thread • Yarn needle • Pins • Stitch markers • Fiberfill for stuffing

HEAD (start in brown yarn)
Rnd 1: start 6 sc in a magic ring [6]
Rnd 2: inc in all 6 st [12]
Rnd 3: (sc in next st, inc in next st) repeat 6 times [18]
Rnd 4: (sc in next st, inc in next st, sc in next st) repeat 6 times [24]
Rnd 5: (sc in next 3 st, inc in next st) repeat 6 times [30]
Rnd 6: (sc in next 2 st, inc in next st, sc in next 2 st) repeat 6 times [36]
Rnd 7: (sc in next 5 st, inc in next st) repeat 6 times [42]
Rnd 8: (sc in next 3 st, inc in next st, sc in next 3 st) repeat 6 times [48]
Rnd 9 – 11: sc in all 48 st [48]
In the next round, we'll alternate between brown and beige yarn. The color change is indicated in italics.
Rnd 12 – 13: sc in next 20 st, *(beige)* sc in next 2 st, *(brown)* sc in next 5 st, *(beige)* sc in next 2 st, *(brown)* sc in next 19 st [48]
Continue crocheting in brown yarn.
Rnd 14 – 18: sc in all 48 st [48] ❶
Insert the safety eyes between rounds 14 and 15, with an interspace of 8 stitches ❷. The beige patches on the head are positioned just above and slightly between the eyes. Stuff the head with fiberfill and continue stuffing as you go.
Rnd 19: (sc in next 3 st, dec, sc in next 3 st) repeat 6 times [42]
Rnd 20: (sc in next 5 st, dec) repeat 6 times [36]
Rnd 21: (sc in next 2 st, dec, sc in next 2 st) repeat 6 times [30]
Rnd 22: (sc in next 4 st, dec, sc in next 4 st) repeat 3 times [27]
Rnd 23 – 25: sc in all 27 st [27]
Rnd 26: (sc in next 4 st, inc in next st, sc in next 4 st) repeat 3 times [30]
Rnd 27: (sc in next 2 st, inc in next st, sc in next 2 st) repeat 6 times [36]
Rnd 28: sc in next 4 st [4] Leave the remaining stitches

unworked.
Fasten off, leaving a yarn tail for sewing. Stuff the head with fiberfill.

SNOUT (in beige yarn)

Leave a starting yarn tail. Ch 4. Stitches are worked around both sides of the foundation chain.
Rnd 1: start in second ch from hook, inc in this ch, sc in next ch, 4 sc in last ch. Continue on the other side of the foundation chain, sc in next ch, inc in last ch [10]
Rnd 2: inc in first st, sc in next 3 st, inc in next 2 st, sc in next 3 st, inc in last st [14]
Rnd 3: (sc in next 3 st, inc in next st, sc in next 3 st) repeat 2 times [16]
Rnd 4: (sc in next 7 st, inc in next st) repeat 2 times [18]
Rnd 5: sc in next 8 st, inc in next st, sc in next 9 st [19]
Rnd 6: sc in next 18 st, inc in next st [20]
Rnd 7: sc in next 9 st, inc in next st, sc in next 10 st [21]
Rnd 8: sc in next 20 st, inc in next st [22]
Rnd 9: sc in next 10 st, inc in next st, sc in next 11 st [23]
Rnd 10: sc in next 22 st, inc in next st [24]
Rnd 11: sc in all 24 st [24]
Rnd 12: sc in next 13 st, ch 1, turn [13] Leave the remaining stitches unworked.
Continue crocheting in rows.
Row 13: skip first sc, sc in next 12 st [12] Leave the remaining stitches unworked (3).
Fasten off, leaving a yarn tail for sewing. Stuff the snout with fiberfill.

SNOUT COVER (in brown yarn)

Ch 5. Crochet in rows.
Row 1: start in second ch from hook, sc in next 4 ch, ch 1, turn [4]
Row 2: sc in next 3 st, inc in next st, ch 1, turn [5]
Row 3: sc in next 4 st, inc in next st, ch 1, turn [6]
Row 4: sc in next 5 st, inc in next st, ch 1, turn [7]
Row 5: sc in next 6 st, inc in next st, ch 1, turn [8]
Row 6: sc in next 7 st, inc in next st, ch 1, turn [9]
Row 7: sc in next 8 st, inc in next st, ch 1, turn [10]
Row 8: sc in next 9 st, inc in next st, ch 1, turn [11]
Row 9: sc in next 10 st, inc in next st [12]
Fasten off, leaving a yarn tail for sewing (4).

EAR (make 2, in brown yarn)

Ch 15. Stitches are worked around both sides of the foundation chain before switching to rows.
Row 1: start in second ch from hook, sc in next 13 ch, 4 sc in last ch. Continue on the other side of the foundation chain, sc in next 13 ch, ch 1, turn [30]
Row 2: sc in next 7 st, hdc in next 3 st, dc inc in next st, dc in next 3 st, dc inc in next 2 st, dc in next 3 st, dc inc in next st, hdc in next 3 st, sc in next 7 st, ch 1, turn [34]
Row 3: sc in next 12 st, hdc inc in next st, hdc in next 3 st, hdc inc in next 2 st, hdc in next 3 st, hdc inc in next st, sc in next 12 st, ch 1, turn [38]
Row 4: sc in next 13 st, (sc in next st, inc in next st) repeat 6 times, sc in next 13 st [44]
Fasten off, leaving a yarn tail for sewing. Slightly stretch the ears to the sides (5).

BODY

Sweater (start in orange yarn)

Rnd 1: start 6 sc in a magic ring [6]
Rnd 2: inc in all 6 st [12]
Rnd 3: (sc in next st, inc in next st) repeat 6 times [18]
Rnd 4: (sc in next st, inc in next st, sc in next st) repeat 6 times [24]
Rnd 5: (sc in next 3 st, inc in next st) repeat 6 times [30]
Rnd 6: (sc in next 2 st, inc in next st, sc in next 2 st) repeat 6 times [36]
Rnd 7: (sc in next 5 st, inc in next st) repeat 6 times [42]
Rnd 8: (sc in next 3 st, inc in next st, sc in next 3 st) repeat 6 times [48]
Rnd 9 – 11: sc in all 48 st [48]
Change to rust yarn.
Rnd 12: sc in all 48 st [48]
In the next rounds, we'll alternate between rust and orange yarn (6). The color change is indicated in italics.

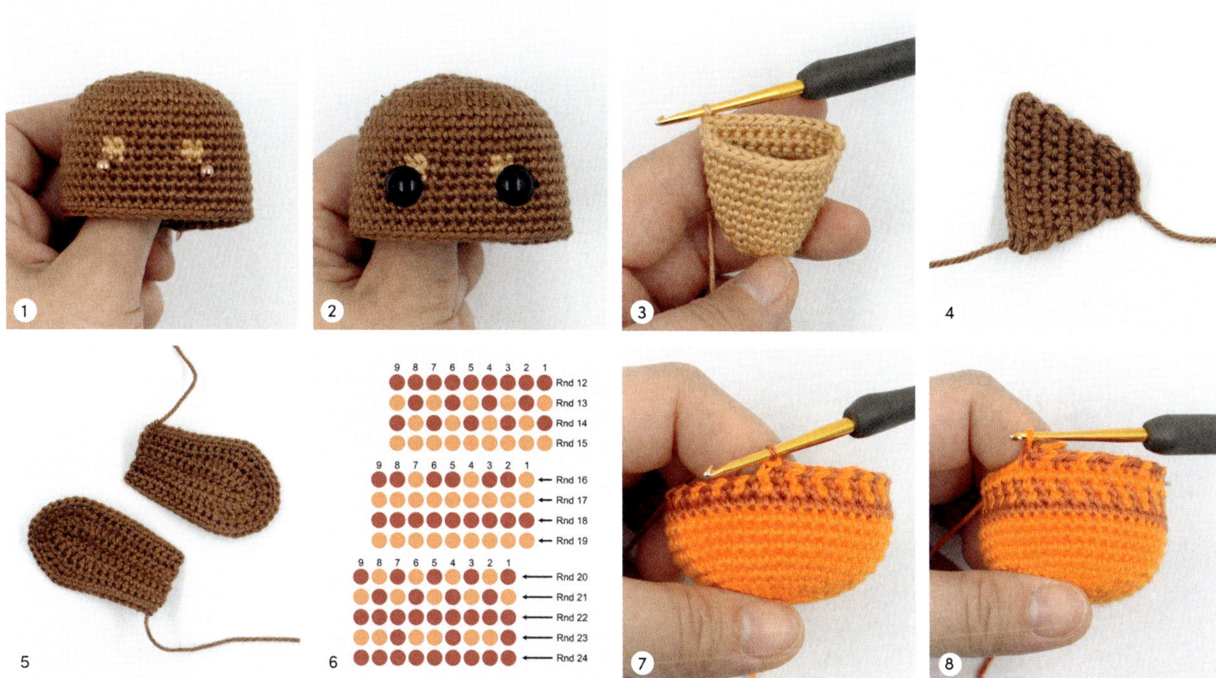

Rnd 13: (*(orange)* sc in next st, *(rust)* sc in next st) repeat 24 times [48]

Rnd 14: (*(rust)* sc in next st, *(orange)* sc in next st) repeat 24 times [48] (7)

Rnd 15: sc in all 48 st [48]

Sc in next st. This is the new start of the round.

Rnd 16: (*(orange)* sc in next st, *(rust)* sc in next 2 st) repeat 16 times [48] (8)

Rnd 17: *(orange)* sc in all 48 st [48]

Rnd 18: *(rust)* sc in all 48 st [48]

Rnd 19: *(orange)* sc in all 48 st [48]

Sc in next st. This is the new start of the round.

Rnd 20: (*(rust)* sc in next st, *(orange)* sc in next st) repeat 24 times [48]

Rnd 21: (*(orange)* sc in next st, *(rust)* sc in next st) repeat 24 times [48]

Rnd 22: *(rust)* sc in all 48 st [48]

Rnd 23: (*(rust)* sc in next st, *(orange)* sc in next 2 st) repeat 16 times [48]

Rnd 24: *(rust)* sc in all 48 st [48]

Sc in next st. This is the new start of the round. Continue crocheting in orange yarn.

Rnd 25: sc in all 48 st [48]

Work the next round in FLO *(and mark the first remaining back loop with a stitch marker)*.

Rnd 26: FLO sc in all 48 st [48] (9)

Rnd 27: sc in all 48 st [48]

Fasten off with an invisible join and weave in the yarn end.

Lower body (in brown yarn)

Pull up a loop of brown yarn in the marked first leftover back loop of the sweater. Fold the hem of the sweater outward to make it easier to access the remaining back loops (9) (10). Work the first stitch in the same stitch where you attached the yarn.

Rnd 1: work this round in BLO, ch 1, sc in next 7 st, (skip next st, sc in next 7 st) repeat 5 times, skip last st [42] (11)

Rnd 2: sc in all 42 st [42]

Stuff the body with fiberfill and continue stuffing as you go.

9

10

11

12

13

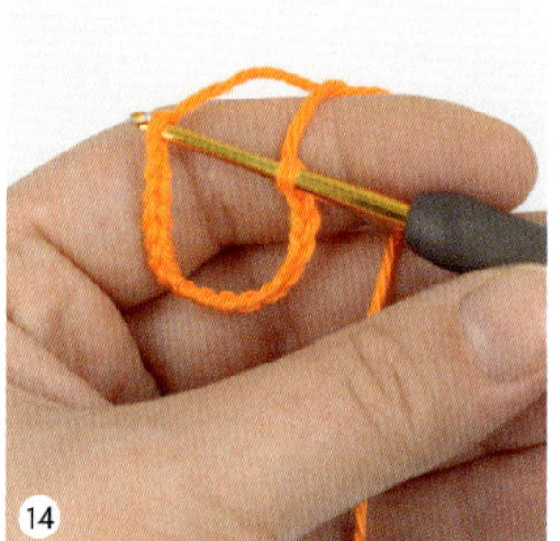
14

15

Rnd 3: (sc in next 19 st, dec) repeat 2 times [40]
Rnd 4: (sc in next 9 st, dec, sc in next 9 st) repeat 2 times [38]
Rnd 5: (sc in next 17 st, dec) repeat 2 times [36]
Rnd 6 – 16: sc in all 36 st [36]
Rnd 17: sc in next 35 st, inc in next st [37]
Rnd 18: sc in next 18 st, inc in next st, sc in next 18 st [38]
Rnd 19: sc in next 37 st, inc in next st [39]
Rnd 20: sc in next 19 st, inc in next st, sc in next 19 st [40]
Rnd 21: sc in next 10 st, inc in next st, sc in next 29 st [41]
Rnd 22: sc in next 30 st, inc in next st, sc in next 10 st [42]
Rnd 23 – 25: sc in all 42 st [42]
Rnd 26: (sc in next 5 st, dec) repeat 6 times [36]
Rnd 27: (sc in next 2 st, dec, sc in next 2 st) repeat 6 times [30]
Rnd 28: (sc in next 3 st, dec) repeat 6 times [24]
Rnd 29: (sc in next st, dec, sc in next st) repeat 6 times [18]
Rnd 30: (sc in next st, dec) repeat 6 times [12]
Rnd 31: dec 6 times [6]
Fasten off, leaving a yarn tail. Using a yarn needle, weave the yarn tail through the front loop of each remaining stitch and pull it tight to close. Weave in the yarn end.

FRONT LEG (make 2, in brown yarn)
Rnd 1: start 6 sc in a magic ring [6]
Rnd 2: inc in all 6 st [12]
Rnd 3 – 7: sc in all 12 st [12]
Rnd 8: sc in all 12 st, ch 1, turn [12]
Continue crocheting in rows.
Row 9: skip first sc, sc in next 7 st, ch 1, turn [7] Leave the remaining stitches unworked.
Row 10: skip first sc, sc in next 6 st, ch 1, turn [6]
Row 11: skip first sc, sc in next 5 st [5]
Fasten off, leaving a yarn tail for sewing. Stuff the front legs with fiberfill 12.

HIND LEG (make 2, in brown yarn)
Rnd 1: start 6 sc in a magic ring [6]
Rnd 2: inc in all 6 st [12]
Rnd 3 – 6: sc in all 12 st [12]

Rnd 7: (sc in next 3 st, inc in next st) repeat 3 times [15]
Rnd 8: (sc in next 2 st, inc in next st, sc in next 2 st) repeat 3 times, ch 1, turn [18]
Continue crocheting in rows.
Row 9: skip first sc, sc in next 11 st, ch 1, turn [11] Leave the remaining stitches unworked.
Row 10: skip first sc, sc in next 10 st, ch 1, turn [10]
Row 11: skip first sc, sc in next 9 st, ch 1, turn [9]
Row 12: skip first sc, sc in next 8 st, ch 1, turn [8]
Row 13: skip first sc, sc in next 7 st, ch 1, turn [7]
Row 14: skip first sc, sc in next st, hdc in next st, dc in next 2 st, hdc in next st, sc in next st [6]
Fasten off, leaving a yarn tail for sewing. Stuff the hind legs with fiberfill 13.

SLEEVE (make 2, in orange yarn)
Ch 18.
Rnd 1: start in first ch to form a circle *(make sure the chains aren't twisted),* sc in all 18 ch [18] 14
Rnd 2: sc in next 15 st, ch 1, turn [15] Leave the remaining stitches unworked.
Continue crocheting in rows.
Rnd 3: skip first sc, sc in next 11 st, ch 1, turn [11] Leave the remaining stitches unworked.
Rnd 4: skip first sc, sc in next 10 st, ch 1, turn [10]
Rnd 5: skip first sc, sc in next 2 st, hdc in next st, dc in next 3 st, hdc in next st, sc in next 2 st [9]
Fasten off, leaving a yarn tail for sewing 15.

TURTLENECK (in rust yarn)
Ch 4. Crochet in rows.
Row 1: start in second ch from hook, sc in next 3 ch, ch 1, turn [3]
Row 2 – 35: BLO sc in next 3 st, ch 1, turn [3]
Row 36: BLO sc in next 3 st [3]
Fasten off, leaving a long tail for sewing 15.

TAIL (in brown yarn)
Rnd 1: start 5 sc in a magic ring [5]
Rnd 2 – 3: sc in all 5 st [5]

16
17
18
19
20
right side up
21
attach the ears here
22
23
24
25
26
27
28

Rnd 4: sc in next 4 st, inc in next st [6]
Rnd 5 – 8: sc in all 6 st [6]
Rnd 9: sc in next 5 st, inc in next st [7]
Rnd 10 – 14: sc in all 7 st [7]
Rnd 15: sc in next 6 st, inc in next st [8]
Rnd 16: sc in all 8 st, ch 1, turn [8]
Continue crocheting in rows.
Row 17: skip first sc, sc in next 4 st, ch 1, turn [4] Leave the remaining stitches unworked.
Row 18: skip first sc, sc in next 3 st [3]
Fasten off, leaving a long tail for sewing.

ASSEMBLY

Assemble the eyes

- Using several strands of white thread, embroider a line along the outer edge of each eye.
- Using black thread, embroider the upper outline (16).

Attach the snout

- Place the snout below the safety eyes with the longer side facing the bottom of the head. Pin the snout in place and sew around using the remaining yarn tail.
- Place the snout cover on top of the snout, pin it in place and sew around using the remaining yarn tail (17).

Embroider the nose

- Using a strand of black embroidery thread, embroider the nose on the top side of the snout tip. The top of the nose should sit on the seam of the snout cover, and the bottom should extend down to the tip of the snout.
- Using the same black thread, embroider a short vertical line below the nose (18).

Attach the ears

- Position the ears on both sides of the head, between rounds 6-14 (19) (20), with the right side facing upward (21). Pin them in place and sew them on using the remaining yarn tails.
- Bend the ears down and sew them to the face to secure the position (22).

Attach the legs

- Place the front legs on rounds 9-13 of the sweater, pointing down. Keep in mind that the color changes of the sweater mark the center of the dog's belly.
- Place the hind legs on the back side of the body, pointing down. They should cover rounds 20-27 of the lower body.
- Pin them in place and check to see if the dog can stand properly. Adjust the position if needed and sew around using the remaining yarn tails (23) (24).

Attach the sleeves

- Put on the sleeves on the dog's front legs. The longer sides of the sleeves (worked in rows) should face outward. Pin them in place and sew around using the remaining yarn tail (25).

Attach the tail

- Pin the tail on rounds 27-30 of the back of the body and sew around using the remaining yarn tail (26).

Attach the head

- Place the head on top of the body. It should cover rounds 8-18 of the sweater. Turn the head slightly to the side to give the dog a cuter look. Pin the head in place and sew around using the remaining yarn tail (27).

Attach the turtleneck

- Wrap the turtleneck around the neck and sew the ends together using the remaining yarn tail. Don't weave in the end yet.
- Pin the turtleneck to the body (leaving some space around the dog's neck) and sew it to the body using the same yarn tail (28).

ROCKY
the French Bulldog

Skill level: ● ● ○
Size: 5" / 12.5 cm tall when made with the indicated yarn.

Amigurumi gallery: Scan or visit www.amigurumi.com/5507 to share pictures and find inspiration.

MATERIALS

• Sport weight yarn in white, black and pink • B-1 / 2.25 mm crochet hook • Safety eyes (11 mm) • Black and white embroidery thread • Yarn needle • Pins • Stitch markers • Fiberfill for stuffing • Optional: white sewing thread *(for the assembly tip)*

HEAD (start in black yarn)

Rnd 1: start 6 sc in a magic ring [6]
Rnd 2: inc in all 6 st [12]
Rnd 3: (sc in next st, inc in next st) repeat 6 times [18]
Rnd 4: (sc in next st, inc in next st, sc in next st) repeat 6 times [24]
Rnd 5: (sc in next 3 st, inc in next st) repeat 6 times [30]
Rnd 6: (sc in next 2 st, inc in next st, sc in next 2 st) repeat 6 times [36]
Rnd 7: (sc in next 5 st, inc in next st) repeat 6 times [42]
Rnd 8: (sc in next 3 st, inc in next st, sc in next 3 st) repeat 6 times [48]
Rnd 9 – 18: sc in all 48 st [48]
Rnd 19: (sc in next 3 st, dec, sc in next 3 st) repeat 6 times [42]
Insert the safety eyes between rounds 13 and 14, with an interspace of 8 stitches. Stuff the head with fiberfill and continue stuffing as you go.
Rnd 20: (sc in next 5 st, dec) repeat 6 times [36]
Rnd 21: (sc in next 2 st, dec, sc in next 2 st) repeat 6 times [30]
Rnd 22: sc in all 30 st [30]
Change to white yarn.
Rnd 23: sc in all 30 st [30]
Rnd 24: (sc in next 2 st, inc in next st, sc in next 2 st) repeat 6 times [36]
Fasten off, leaving a yarn tail for sewing (1).

SNOUT

Base (in white yarn)
Leave a starting yarn tail. Ch 5. Stitches are worked around both sides of the foundation chain.
Rnd 1: start in second ch from hook, inc in this ch, sc in next 2 ch, 4 sc in last ch. Continue on the other side of the foundation chain, sc in next 2 ch, inc in last ch [12]

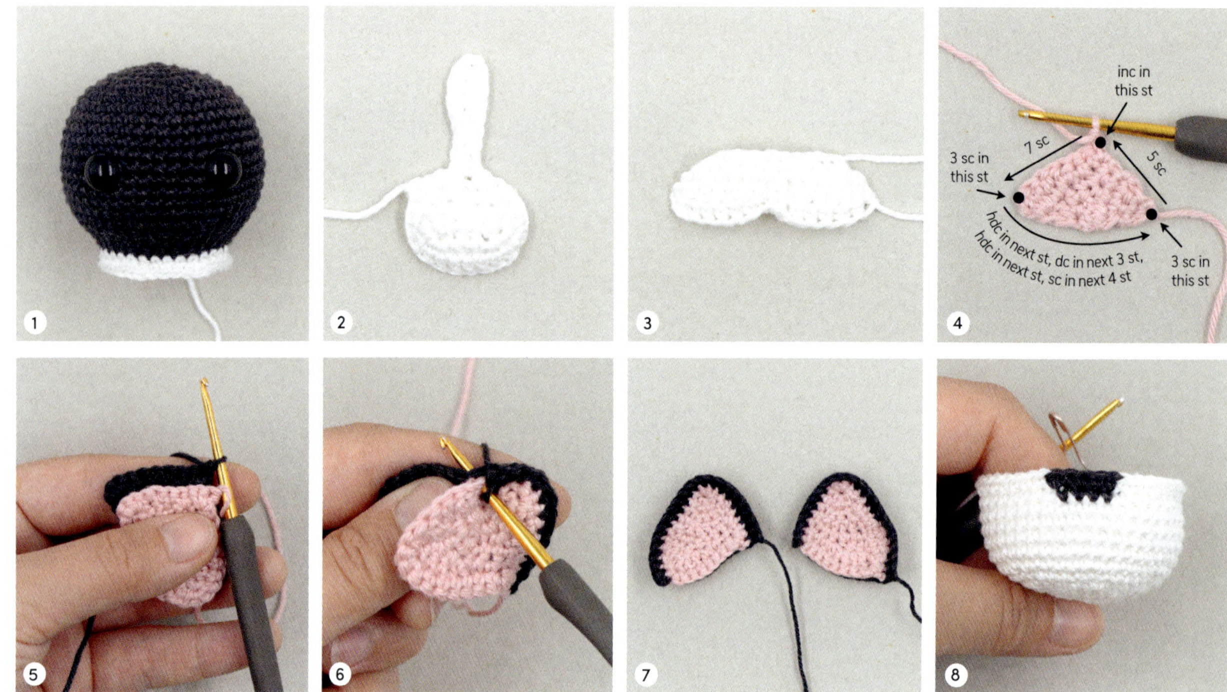

Rnd 2: inc in next 2 st, sc in next 2 st, inc in next 4 st, sc in next 2 st, inc in next 2 st [20]
Using a yarn needle, weave the starting yarn tail through the foundation chain to hide the stitch gaps.
In the next round, we'll start making the stripe that covers the puppy's forehead.
Rnd 3: sc in next 2 st, hdc inc in next st, dc in next 5 st, hdc inc in next st, sc in next 6 st, ch 10, start in third ch from hook, dc in next 3 ch, hdc in next 2 ch, sc in next 3 ch, continue on the snout, skip 1 st, sc in next 4 st [29]
Fasten off, leaving a yarn tail for sewing 2.

Cover (in white yarn)
Ch 11. Crochet in rows.
Row 1: start in second ch from hook, sc in next 10 ch, ch 2, turn [10]
Row 2: 3 dc in next st, dc in next 3 st, ch 1, sc in next 2 st, ch 1, dc in next 3 st, 3 dc in last st, ch 2, turn [14]
Row 3: hdc in next 6 st, ch 1, sc in next 2 st, ch 1, hdc in next 6 st [14]
Fasten off, leaving a yarn tail for sewing 3.

EYELID (make 2, in black yarn)
Ch 4. Fasten off and leave a yarn tail for sewing.

RIGHT EAR

Inner part (in pink yarn)
Ch 2. Crochet in rows.
Row 1: start in second ch from hook, inc in this ch, ch 1, turn [2]
Row 2: sc in next st, inc in next st, ch 1, turn [3]
Row 3: sc in next 2 st, inc in next st, ch 2, turn [4]
Row 4: dc inc in next st, hdc in next st, sc in next 2 st, ch 1, turn [5]
Row 5: sc in next 3 st, hdc in next st, dc inc in last st, ch 2, turn [6]
Row 6: dc inc in next st, dc in next st, hdc inc in next st,

sc in next 3 st [8]
Next, we crochet around the ear ④.
Row 7: ch 1, turn, sc in next 7 st, 3 sc in next st, continue in the row-ends on the longer side of the ear, hdc in next st, dc in next 3 st, hdc in next st, sc in next 4 st, 3 sc in next st, continue in the row-ends on the shorter side of the ear, sc in next 5 st, inc in next st [29]
Fasten off and set aside.

Outer part (in black yarn)
Ch 2. Crochet in rows.
Row 1 – 7: repeat the instructions for the inner part, but don't fasten off.
In the next row, we'll join the inner and outer parts together.
Row 8: ch 1, turn, place the inner part on top of your work with the wrong side facing up and crochet through both layers ⑤ ⑥, sc in next 21 st, ch 1, turn [21] Leave the remaining stitches unworked.
Row 9: sc in all 21 st [21]
Fasten off, leaving a yarn tail for sewing. Weave in all other yarn ends.

LEFT EAR

Inner part (in pink yarn)
Ch 2. Crochet in rows.
Row 1: start in second ch from hook, inc in this ch, ch 1, turn [2]
Row 2: sc in next st, inc in next st, ch 1, turn [3]
Row 3: sc in next 2 st, inc in next st, ch 1, turn [4]
Row 4: sc in next 2 st, hdc in next st, dc inc in last st, ch 2, turn [5]
Row 5: dc inc in first st, hdc in next st, sc in next 3 st, ch 1, turn [6]
Row 6: sc in next 3 st, hdc inc in next st, dc in next st, dc inc in last st [8]
Next, we crochet around the ear.
Row 7: ch 1, turn, sc in next 7 st, 3 sc in next st, continue in the row-ends on the shorter side of the ear, sc in next 5 st, 3 sc in next st, continue in the row-ends on the longer side of the ear, sc in next 4 st, hdc in next st, dc in next 3 st, hdc in next st, inc in next st [29]
Fasten off and set aside.

Outer part (in black yarn)
Ch 2. Crochet in rows.
Row 1 – 7: repeat the instructions for the inner part, but don't fasten off.
In the next row, we'll join the inner and outer parts together.
Row 8: ch 1, turn, place the inner part on top of your work with the wrong side facing up and crochet through both layers, sc in next 21 st, ch 1, turn [21] Leave the remaining stitches unworked.
Row 9: sc in all 21 st [21]
Fasten off, leaving a black yarn tail for sewing. Weave in the other yarn ends ⑦.

BODY (start in white yarn)

Rnd 1: start 6 sc in a magic ring [6]
Rnd 2: inc in all 6 st [12]
Rnd 3: (sc in next st, inc in next st) repeat 6 times [18]
Rnd 4: (sc in next st, inc in next st, sc in next st) repeat 6 times [24]
Rnd 5: (sc in next 3 st, inc in next st) repeat 6 times [30]
Rnd 6: (sc in next 2 st, inc in next st, sc in next 2 st) repeat 6 times [36]
Rnd 7: (sc in next 5 st, inc in next st) repeat 6 times [42]
Rnd 8 – 11: sc in all 42 st [42]
In the next rounds, we'll alternate between white and black yarn. The color change is indicated in italics.
Rnd 12: sc in next 19 st, *(black)* sc in next 4 st, *(white)* sc in next 19 st [42]
Rnd 13: sc in next 19 st, *(black)* sc in next 5 st, *(white)* sc in next 18 st [42] ⑧
Rnd 14: sc in next 18 st, *(black)* sc in next 6 st, *(white)* sc in next 18 st [42]
Rnd 15: sc in next 17 st, *(black)* sc in next 8 st, *(white)* sc in next 17 st [42]
Rnd 16: (sc in next 5 st, dec) repeat 2 times, sc in next st, *(black)* sc in next 4 st, dec, sc in next 5 st, dec, *(white)* (sc in

9

10

11

12

next 5 st, dec) repeat 2 times [36]
Rnd 17: sc in next 8 st, dec, sc in next 2 st, *(black)* sc in next 14 st, *(white)* dec, sc in next 8 st [34]
Rnd 18: sc in next 9 st, *(black)* sc in next 6 st, dec, sc in next 9 st, *(white)* sc in next 6 st, dec [32]
Rnd 19: sc in next 7 st, dec, *(black)* sc in next 14 st, dec, *(white)* sc in next 7 st [30]
Rnd 20: sc in next 8 st, *(black)* sc in next 15 st, *(white)* sc in next 7 st [30]
Rnd 21: sc in next 9 st, *(black)* sc in next 13 st, *(white)* sc in next 8 st [30]
Rnd 22: sc in next 9 st, inc in next st, *(black)* sc in next 9 st, inc in next st, sc in next st, *(white)* sc in next 8 st, inc in next st [33]
Rnd 23: sc in next 5 st, inc in next st, sc in next 7 st, *(black)* sc in next 3 st, inc in next st, sc in next 6 st, *(white)* sc in next 4 st, inc in next st, sc in next 5 st [36]
Stuff the body with fiberfill and continue stuffing as you go.
Rnd 24: sc in next 15 st, *(black)* sc in next 11 st, *(white)* sc in next 10 st [36]
Rnd 25: sc in next 16 st, *(black)* sc in next 11 st, *(white)* sc in next 9 st [36]
Rnd 26: sc in next 20 st, *(black)* sc in next 7 st, *(white)* sc in next 9 st [36]
Rnd 27: sc in next 22 st, *(black)* sc in next 4 st, *(white)* sc in next 10 st [36]
Rnd 28: (sc in next 2 st, dec, sc in next 2 st) repeat 3 times, sc in next 2 st, dec, sc in next st, *(black)* sc in next 2 st, *(white)* sc in next st, dec, sc in next 4 st, dec, sc in next 2 st [30]
Continue crocheting in white yarn.
Rnd 29: (sc in next 3 st, dec) repeat 3 times, sc in next st, dec, sc in next 2 st, (sc in next 3 st, dec) repeat 2 times [24]
Rnd 30: (sc in next st, dec, sc in next st) repeat 6 times [18]
Rnd 31: (sc in next st, dec) repeat 6 times [12]
Rnd 32: dec 6 times [6]
Fasten off, leaving a yarn tail. Using a yarn needle, weave the yarn tail through the front loop of each remaining stitch and pull it tight to close. Weave in the yarn end (9).

TAIL (in white yarn)
Rnd 1: start 6 sc in a magic ring [6]
Rnd 2: (sc in next st, inc in next st) repeat 3 times [9]
Rnd 3: sc in all 9 st [9]
Fasten off, leaving a yarn tail for sewing. You can add some fiberfill to the tail, but stuffing is optional.

FRONT LEG (make 2, in white yarn)
Rnd 1: start 6 sc in a magic ring [6]
Rnd 2: (sc in next st, inc in next st) repeat 3 times [9]
Rnd 3 – 5: sc in all 9 st [9]
Rnd 6: sc in next 4 st, inc in next st, sc in next 4 st [10]
Rnd 7: sc in next 9 st, inc in next st [11]
Rnd 8: sc in all 11 st [11]
Rnd 9: sc in next 5 st, inc in next st, sc in next 5 st [12]
Rnd 10: sc in all 12 st, ch 1, turn [12]
Continue crocheting in rows.
Row 11: skip first sc, sc in next 7 st, ch 1, turn [7] Leave the remaining stitches unworked.

Row 12: skip first sc, sc in next 6 st, ch 1, turn [6]
Row 13: skip first sc, sc in next 5 st, ch 1, turn [5]
Row 14: skip first sc, sc in next 4 st, ch 1, turn [4]
Row 15: skip first sc, sc in next 3 st [3]
Fasten off, leaving a yarn tail for sewing. Stuff the front legs with fiberfill (10).

HIND LEG (make 2)

Upper part (in white yarn)

Rnd 1: start 7 sc in a magic ring [7]
Rnd 2: inc in all 7 st [14]
Rnd 3: (sc in next st, inc in next st) repeat 7 times [21]
Rnd 4: (sc in next st, inc in next st, sc in next st) repeat 7 times [28]
Rnd 5: (sc in next 3 st, inc in next st) repeat 7 times [35]
Rnd 6: sc in all 35 st [35]
Rnd 7: (sc in next 3 st, dec) repeat 7 times [28]
Rnd 8: (sc in next st, dec, sc in next st) repeat 7 times [21]
Stuff lightly with fiberfill. The upper part of the leg should have some volume, but also remain quite flat.
Rnd 9: (sc in next st, dec) repeat 7 times [14]
Rnd 10: dec 7 times [7]
Fasten off, leaving a yarn tail. Using a yarn needle, weave the yarn tail through the front loop of each remaining stitch and pull it tight to close. Leave a yarn tail for sewing (11).

Foot (in white yarn)

Rnd 1: start 6 sc in a magic ring [6]
Rnd 2: (sc in next st, inc in next st) repeat 3 times [9]
Rnd 3 – 4: sc in all 9 st [9]
Rnd 5: sc in all 9 st, ch 1, turn [9]
Continue crocheting in rows.
Row 6: skip first sc, sc in next 5 st, ch 1, turn [5] Leave the remaining stitches unworked.
Row 7: skip first sc, sc in next 4 st, ch 1, turn [4]
Row 8: skip first sc, sc in next 3 st [3]
Fasten off, leaving a yarn tail for sewing. Stuff the feet with fiberfill (12).

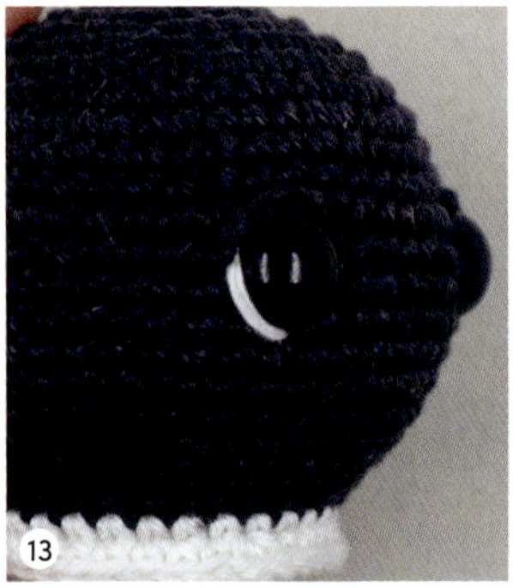

13 14 15 16

17 18 19 20

21 22 23 24

ASSEMBLY

TIP: Sewing white pieces onto the black parts can be challenging. To make the seams less noticeable, try using white sewing thread and a thin needle instead of the yarn tails.

Assemble the eyes

- Using several strands of white thread, embroider a line along the outer edge of each eye 13.
- Sew the eyelids above the safety eyes 13.

Attach the snout

- Pin the snout in place just below the safety eyes, aligning the stripe with the center of the forehead. Sew it on using the remaining yarn tail 14. Stuff lightly with fiberfill before closing the seam.
- Place the snout cover on top of the base with the foundation chain on the top side. Pin it in place and sew around using the

remaining yarn tail (15).

- Using black thread, embroider a nose on round 2 of the snout cover, a short vertical line below the nose and some dots on both sides of the snout (16).

Attach the ears

- Position the ears on both sides of the head, between rounds 3-15 (17) (18). Pin them in place and sew them on using the remaining yarn tails (19).

Attach the front legs

- Place the front legs on the front (wider) side of the body, covering rounds 9-13. Be sure the black patch remains centered on the back of the body.
- Pin them in place and check to see if the puppy can sit properly. Adjust the position if needed and sew around using the remaining yarn tails (20) (21).

Attach the hind legs

- Place the upper parts of the hind legs on the lower sides of the body. It's easiest to do this while your dog is sitting on a flat surface. The upper parts should cover rounds 20-29 of the body and extend slightly toward the front. Pin them in place and sew around using the remaining yarn tails (22).
- Place the feet below the upper parts of the hind legs. The feet should be facing the front side of the dog. Pin them in place and sew around using the remaining yarn tails (23).

Attach the tail

- Position the tail to the back of the body, right below the black patch. Pin it in place and sew around using the remaining yarn tail (24).

Attach the head

- Place the head on top of the neck. Turn the head slightly to the side to give your dog a cuter look. Pin it in place and sew around using the remaining yarn tail.

TACO
the Calico Cat

Skill level: 
Size: 5.1" / 13 cm tall when made with the indicated yarn.

Amigurumi gallery: Scan or visit www.amigurumi.com/5508 to share pictures and find inspiration.

MATERIALS

• Sport weight yarn in orange, black, white and pink • B-1 / 2.25 mm crochet hook • Safety eyes (11 mm) • White sewing thread *(for the whiskers)* • Black, green and pink embroidery thread • Yarn needle • Pins • Stitch markers • Fiberfill for stuffing • Approx. 4" / 10 cm of wire or pipe cleaner *(for the tail)*

HEAD (start in black yarn)

Rnd 1: start 6 sc in a magic ring [6]

Rnd 2: inc in all 6 st [12]

Rnd 3: (sc in next st, inc in next st) repeat 6 times [18]

Rnd 4: (sc in next st, inc in next st, sc in next st) repeat 6 times [24]

Rnd 5: (sc in next 3 st, inc in next st) repeat 6 times [30]

In the next rounds, we'll alternate between black and orange yarn. The color change is indicated in italics.

Rnd 6: (sc in next 2 st, inc in next st, sc in next 2 st) repeat 3 times, *(orange)* sc in next st, *(black)* sc in next st, inc in next st, sc in next 2 st, (sc in next 2 st, inc in next st, sc in next 2 st) repeat 2 times [36]

Rnd 7: (sc in next 5 st, inc) repeat 2 times, sc in next 5 st, *(orange)* inc in next st, sc in next st, *(black)* sc in next 4 st, inc in next st, (sc in next 5 st, inc in next st) repeat 2 times [42]

Rnd 8: (sc in next 3 st, inc in next st, sc in next 3 st) repeat 2 times, sc in next 3 st, inc in next st, *(orange)* sc in next 5 st, *(black)* sc in next st, inc in next st, sc in next 3 st, (sc in next 3 st, inc in next st, sc in next 3 st) repeat 2 times [48]

Rnd 9: sc in next 20 st, *(orange)* sc in next 6 st, *(black)* sc in next 22 st [48]

Rnd 10: sc in next 18 st, *(orange)* sc in next 7 st, *(black)* sc in next 23 st [48]

Rnd 11 – 12: sc in next 17 st, *(orange)* sc in next 8 st, *(black)* sc in next 23 st [48]

Rnd 13 – 14: sc in next 16 st, *(orange)* sc in next 8 st, *(black)* sc in next 24 st [48]

In the next rounds, we'll alternate between black, orange and white yarn. The color change is indicated in italics.

Rnd 15: sc in next 17 st, *(orange)* sc in next 6 st, *(white)* sc in next 5 st, *(black)* sc in next 20 st [48]

Rnd 16: sc in next 18 st, *(orange)* sc in next 4 st, *(white)* sc in next 7 st, *(black)* sc in next 19 st [48]
Rnd 17: (sc in next 3 st, dec, sc in next 3 st) repeat 2 times, sc in next 3 st, dec, *(white)* sc in next 6 st, dec, sc in next 2 st, *(black)* sc in next st, (sc in next 3 st, dec, sc in next 3 st) repeat 2 times [42]
Rnd 18: (sc in next 5 st, dec) repeat 2 times, sc in next 3 st, *(white)* sc in next 2 st, dec, sc in next 4 st, dec, sc in next st, *(black)* (sc in next 5 st, dec) repeat 2 times [36]
The center of the white patch is the center of the cat's face ①. Insert the safety eyes between rounds 13-14, with an interspace of 9 stitches ②.
Stuff the head with fiberfill and continue stuffing as you go.
Rnd 19: (sc in next 2 st, dec, sc in next 2 st) repeat 2 times, sc in next st, *(white)* sc in next st, dec, sc in next 4 st, dec, sc in next 4 st, *(black)* sc in next st, dec, sc in next 3 st, dec, sc in next 2 st [30]
Rnd 20: (sc in next 3 st, dec) repeat 2 times, *(white)* (sc in next 3 st, dec) repeat 3 times, *(black)* sc in next 3 st, dec [24]
Rnd 21: sc in next 8 st, *(white)* sc in next 16 st [24]
Continue crocheting in white yarn.
Rnd 22: sc in all 24 st [24]
Rnd 23: (sc in next 3 st, inc in next st) repeat 6 times [30]
Fasten off, leaving a yarn tail for sewing.

SNOUT (in white yarn)
Rnd 1: start 7 sc in a magic ring [7]
Rnd 2: inc in all 7 st [14]
Rnd 3: sc in next 10 st, hdc inc in next st, dc in next 3 st [15]
In the next round, we'll start making the stripe that covers the cat's forehead.
Rnd 4: dc in next 2 st, hdc inc in next st, sc in next 4 st, ch 6, start in third ch from hook, hdc in next 2 ch, sc in next 2 ch, continue on the snout, sc in next 6 st [18] Leave the remaining stitches unworked.
Fasten off, leaving a yarn tail for sewing.

Attach the whiskers

Prepare 4 strands of white sewing thread, each about 6" / 15 cm long. Note that the stripe marks the top center of the snout. With the wrong side of the snout facing you, tie 2 strands on the left and 2 strands on the right, keeping the knots on the inside so they remain hidden from the front 3. Each knot creates 2 loose ends, giving you 4 strands on each side. Pull each strand through a separate stitch gap to the front side of the snout 4.

RIGHT EAR

Inner part (in pink yarn)

Ch 2. Crochet in rows.
Row 1: start in second ch from hook, inc in this ch, ch 1, turn [2]
Row 2: sc in next st, inc in next st, ch 1, turn [3]
Row 3: sc in next 2 st, inc in next st, ch 2, turn [4]
Row 4: dc inc in next st, hdc in next st, sc in next 2 st, ch 1, turn [5]
Row 5: sc in next 2 st, hdc in next st, dc in next st, dc inc in next st, ch 2, turn [6]
Row 6: dc inc in next st, dc in next st, hdc inc in next st, sc in next 3 st [8]
Next, we crochet around the ear 5.
Row 7: ch 1, turn, sc in next 7 st, 3 sc in next st, continue in the row-ends on the longer side of the ear, sc in next 8 st, 3 sc in next st, continue in the row-ends on the shorter side of the ear, sc in next 5 st, inc in next st [28]
Fasten off and set aside.

Outer part (in orange yarn)

Ch 2. Crochet in rows.
Row 1 – 7: repeat the instructions for the inner part, but don't fasten off.
In the next row, we'll join the inner and outer parts together.
Row 8: ch 1, turn, place the inner part on top of your work with the wrong side facing up and crochet through both layers 6 7, sc in next 20 st, ch 1, turn [20] Leave the remaining stitches unworked.
Row 9: sc in all 20 st [20]
Fasten off, leaving an orange yarn tail for sewing. Weave in all other yarn ends.

LEFT EAR

Inner part (in pink yarn)

Ch 2. Crochet in rows.
Row 1: start in second ch from hook, inc in this ch, ch 1, turn [2]
Row 2: sc in next st, inc in next st, ch 1, turn [3]
Row 3: sc in next 2 st, inc in next st, ch 1, turn [4]
Row 4: sc in next 2 st, hdc in next st, dc inc in next st, ch 2, turn [5]
Row 5: dc inc in next st, dc in next st, hdc in next st, sc in next 2 st, ch 1, turn [6]
Row 6: sc in next 3 st, hdc inc in next st, dc in next st, dc inc in next st [8]
Next, we crochet around the ear.
Row 7: ch 1, turn, sc in next 7 st, 3 sc in next st, continue in the row-ends on the shorter side of the ear, sc in next 5 st, 3 sc in next st, continue in the row-ends on the longer side of the ear, sc in next 8 st, inc in next st [28]
Fasten off and set aside.

Outer part (in black yarn)

Ch 2. Crochet in rows.
Row 1 – 7: repeat the instructions for the inner part, but don't fasten off.
In the next row, we'll join the inner and outer parts together.
Row 8: ch 1, turn, place the inner part on top of your work with the wrong side facing up and crochet through both layers, sc in next 20 st, ch 1, turn [20] Leave the remaining stitches unworked.
Row 9: sc in all 20 st [20]
Fasten off, leaving a black yarn tail for sewing. Weave in all other yarn ends 8.

BODY (start in white yarn)

Rnd 1: start 6 sc in a magic ring [6]
Rnd 2: inc in all 6 st [12]
Rnd 3: (sc in next st, inc in next st) repeat 6 times [18]

9

10

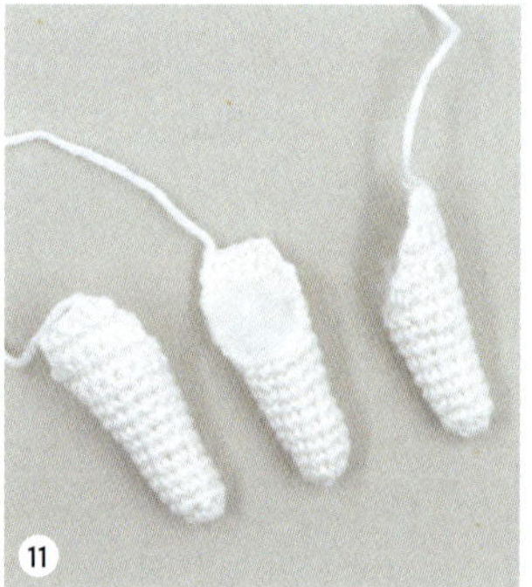
11

12

Rnd 4: (sc in next st, inc in next st, sc in next st) repeat 6 times [24]
Rnd 5: (sc in next 3 st, inc in next st) repeat 6 times [30]
Rnd 6: (sc in next 2 st, inc in next st, sc in next 2 st) repeat 6 times [36]
Rnd 7 – 10: sc in all 36 st [36]
In the next rounds, we'll alternate between white, orange and black yarn. The color change is indicated in italics.
Rnd 11: sc in next 6 st, *(orange)* sc in next 4 st, *(white)* sc in next 26 st [36]
Rnd 12: sc in next 6 st, *(orange)* sc in next 6 st, *(white)* sc in next 24 st [36]
Rnd 13: sc in next 4 st, dec, sc in next st, *(orange)* sc in next 3 st, *(black)* sc in next 5 st, *(white)* sc in next 2 st, dec, sc in next 10 st, dec, sc in next 5 st [33]
Rnd 14: sc in next 7 st, *(orange)* sc in next 2 st, *(black)* sc in next st, dec, sc in next 3 st, *(white)* sc in next 3 st, *(orange)* sc in next 2 st, *(white)* dec, sc in next 9 st, dec [30]
Rnd 15: sc in next 8 st, *(orange)* sc in next 3 st, *(black)* sc in next 3 st, *(white)* sc in next 2 st, *(orange)* sc in next 5 st, *(white)* sc in next 9 st [30]
Rnd 16: sc in next 7 st, *(black)* sc in next 2 st, *(orange)* sc in next 4 st, *(black)* sc in next 2 st, *(white)* sc in next 3 st, *(black)* sc in next 2 st, *(orange)* sc in next 3 st, *(white)* sc in next 7 st [30] 9
Rnd 17: sc in next 7 st, *(black)* sc in next 7 st, *(white)* sc in next 4 st, *(black)* sc in next 3 st, *(orange)* sc in next 2 st, *(white)* sc in next 7 st [30]
Rnd 18: sc in next 4 st, inc in next st, sc in next 3 st, *(black)* sc in next st, inc in next st, sc in next 4 st, inc in next st, *(orange)* sc in next 4 st, inc in next st, sc in next 2 st, *(white)* sc in next 2 st, inc in next st, sc in next 4 st, inc in next st [36]
Rnd 19: sc in next 10 st, *(black)* sc in next 8 st, *(orange)* sc in next 8 st, *(white)* sc in next 10 st [36]
Rnd 20: sc in next 9 st, *(black)* sc in next 3 st, *(orange)* sc in next 2 st, *(black)* sc in next 3 st, *(orange)* sc in next 8 st, *(white)* sc in next 11 st [36]
Stuff the body with fiberfill and continue stuffing as you go.
Rnd 21: sc in next 9 st, *(orange)* sc in next 5 st, *(black)* sc in next 3 st, *(orange)* sc in next 6 st, *(white)* sc in next 13 st [36]
Rnd 22: sc in next 8 st, *(orange)* sc in next 7 st, *(black)* sc in next 4 st, *(orange)* sc in next 3 st, *(white)* sc in next 14 st [36]
Rnd 23: sc in next 6 st, *(orange)* sc in next 10 st, *(black)* sc in next 4 st, *(orange)* sc in next 2 st, *(white)* sc in next 14 st [36]
Rnd 24: sc in next 2 st, dec, sc in next 2 st, *(orange)* (sc in next 2 st, dec, sc in next 2 st) repeat 2 times, *(black)* sc in next 2 st, dec, sc in next 2 st, *(white)* (sc in next 2 st, dec, sc in next 2 st) repeat 2 times [30]
Rnd 25: sc in next 3 st, dec, *(orange)* (sc in next 3 st, dec) repeat 2 times, *(black)* sc in next 3 st, dec, *(white)* (sc in next 3 st, dec) repeat 2 times [24]
Rnd 26: sc in next st, dec, sc in next 2 st, *(orange)* (dec, sc in next 2 st) repeat 2 times, dec, *(white)* (sc in next 2 st, dec) repeat 2 times, sc in next st [18]
Continue crocheting in white yarn.
Rnd 27: (sc in next st, dec) repeat 6 times [12]
Rnd 28: dec 6 times [6]
Fasten off, leaving a yarn tail for sewing 10.

LEG IN ONE COLOR (make 3, in white yarn)
Rnd 1: start 6 sc in a magic ring [6]
Rnd 2: (sc in next st, inc in next st) repeat 3 times [9]
Rnd 3 – 5: sc in all 9 st [9]
Rnd 6: sc in next 4 st, inc in next st, sc in next 4 st [10]
Rnd 7: sc in next 9 st, inc in next st [11]
Rnd 8: sc in next 5 st, inc in next st, sc in next 5 st [12]
Rnd 9: sc in next 11 st, inc in next st [13]
Rnd 10: sc in next 6 st, inc in next st, sc in next 6 st, ch 1, turn [14]
Continue crocheting in rows.
Row 11: skip first sc, sc in next 8 st, ch 1, turn [8] Leave the remaining stitches unworked.
Row 12: skip first sc, sc in next 7 st, ch 1, turn [7]
Row 13: skip first sc, sc in next 6 st, ch 1, turn [6]
Row 14: skip first sc, sc in next 5 st, ch 1, turn [5]
Row 15: skip first sc, sc in next 4 st [4]
Fasten off, leaving a yarn tail for sewing. Stuff the legs with fiberfill (11).

COLORED LEG (start in black yarn)
Rnd 1: start 6 sc in a magic ring [6]
Rnd 2: (sc in next st, inc in next st) repeat 3 times [9]
Rnd 3: sc in all 9 st [9]
In the next rounds, we'll alternate between black and orange yarn. The color change is indicated in italics.
Rnd 4: sc in next 5 st, *(orange)* sc in next 4 st [9]
Rnd 5: *(black)* sc in next 5 st, *(orange)* sc in next 4 st [9]
Rnd 6: sc in next 2 st, *(black)* sc in next 2 st, inc in next st, sc in next 2 st, *(orange)* sc in next 2 st [10]
Rnd 7: sc in next 5 st, *(black)* sc in next 3 st, *(orange)* sc in next st, inc in next st [11]
Rnd 8: sc in next 5 st, inc in next st, *(black)* sc in next 3 st, *(orange)* sc in next 2 st [12]
Continue crocheting in orange yarn.
Rnd 9: sc in next 11 st, inc in next st [13]
Rnd 10: sc in next 6 st, inc in next st, sc in next 6 st, ch 1, turn [14]
Continue crocheting in rows.
Row 11: skip first sc, sc in next 8 st, ch 1, turn [8] Leave the

remaining stitches unworked.
Row 12: skip first sc, sc in next 7 st, ch 1, turn [7]
Row 13: skip first sc, sc in next 6 st, ch 1, turn [6]
Row 14: skip first sc, sc in next 5 st, ch 1, turn [5]
Row 15: skip first sc, sc in next 4 st [4]
Fasten off, leaving a yarn tail for sewing. Stuff the leg with fiberfill (12).

TAIL (start in white yarn)
Rnd 1: start 6 sc in a magic ring [6]
Rnd 2: sc in all 6 st [6]
Rnd 3: sc in next 5 st, inc in next st [7]
Rnd 4: sc in next 3 st, inc in next st, sc in next 3 st [8]
Rnd 5 – 17: sc in all 8 st [8]
In the next rounds, we'll alternate between white and black yarn. The color change is indicated in italics.
Rnd 18: sc in next 3 st, *(black)* sc in next 2 st, *(white)* sc in

next 3 st [8]
Rnd 19: sc in next 2 st, *(black)* sc in next 4 st, *(white)* sc in next 2 st [8]
Rnd 20: sc in next st, *(black)* sc in next 7 st [8]
Continue crocheting in black yarn.
Rnd 21: sc in next 3 st, ch 1, turn [3] Leave the remaining stitches unworked.
Continue crocheting in rows.
Row 22: skip first sc, sc in next 4 st, ch 1, turn [4] Leave the remaining stitches unworked.
Row 23: skip first sc, sc in next 3 st [3]
Fasten off, leaving a yarn tail for sewing.

ASSEMBLY

Make the eyes colorful

- Using several strands of green thread, embroider a line along the outer edge of each eye (14).
- Using black thread, embroider the upper outline and eyelashes (14).

Attach the snout

- Pin the snout in place just below the safety eyes, aligning the stripe with the center of the forehead. Sew it on using the remaining yarn tail. Stuff with fiberfill before closing the seam (15).
- Using pink thread, embroider a nose between rounds 2-3 on the top side of the snout. Then add a short vertical line below the nose to create a T-shape (16).
- Cut the whiskers to the desired length. You get the cutest look when each whisker is a slightly different length.

Attach the ears

- Position the ears on both sides of the head, between rounds 3-14 (17) (18). Pin them in place and sew them on using the remaining yarn tails (19).

Attach the legs

- Place the legs on the lower side of the body (20) (21) (22). The colored leg (left hind leg) should be positioned on the orange patch. Pin them in place and check to see if the cat can stand properly. Adjust the position if needed and sew around using the remaining yarn tails.

Attach the head

- Place the head on top of the body. It should cover rounds 4-14. Turn the head slightly to the left side. Pin the head in place and sew around using the remaining yarn tail (23).

Attach the tail

- Insert the piece of wire or the pipe cleaner inside the tail.
- Pin the tail at the back side of the body, pointing upward, and sew around using the remaining yarn tail (24).

BELLA
the German Shepherd

Skill level: ● ● ○
Size: 6" / 15 cm tall when made with the indicated yarn.

Amigurumi gallery: Scan or visit www.amigurumi.com/5509 to share pictures and find inspiration.

MATERIALS

- Sport weight yarn in amber, brown and light brown • B-1 / 2.25 mm crochet hook • Safety eyes (11 mm)
- Black and white embroidery thread • Yarn needle • Pins • Stitch markers • Fiberfill for stuffing
- Optional: Approx. 3.2" / 8 cm of wire or pipe cleaner *(for the tail if you want it to be posable)*

HEAD (start in brown yarn)

Rnd 1: start 6 sc in a magic ring [6]

Rnd 2: inc in all 6 st [12]

Rnd 3: (sc in next st, inc in next st) repeat 6 times [18]

Rnd 4: (sc in next st, inc in next st, sc in next st) repeat 6 times [24]

Change to amber yarn. In the next rounds, we'll alternate between amber and brown yarn. The color change is indicated in italics.

Rnd 5: sc in next 3 st, inc in next st, *(brown)* sc in next 3 st, inc in next st, *(amber)* sc in next 3 st, inc in next st, sc in next st, *(brown)* sc in next 2 st, inc in next st, sc in next st, *(amber)* sc in next 2 st, inc in next st, sc in next 3 st, inc in next st [30] 1

Rnd 6: sc in next 2 st, inc in next st, sc in next 2 st, *(brown)* sc in next 2 st, inc in next st, sc in next 3 st, *(amber)* sc in next st, inc in next st, sc in next 2 st, *(brown)* sc in next 2 st, inc in next st, sc in next 3 st, *(amber)* sc in next st, inc in next st, sc in next 4 st, inc in next st, sc in next 2 st [36]

Rnd 7: sc in next 5 st, inc in next st, *(brown)* sc in next 5 st, inc in next st, *(amber)* sc in next 5 st, inc in next st, sc in next st, *(brown)* sc in next 4 st, inc in next st, sc in next st, *(amber)* sc in next 4 st, inc in next st, sc in next 5 st, inc in next st [42] 2

Rnd 8: sc in next 3 st, inc in next st, sc in next 5 st, *(brown)* sc in next st, inc in next st, sc in next 2 st, *(amber)* sc in next 4 st, inc in next st, sc in next 5 st, *(brown)* sc in next st, inc in next st, sc in next 2 st, *(amber)* sc in next 4 st, inc in next st, sc in next 6 st, inc in next st, sc in next 3 st [48]

Rnd 9: sc in next 16 st, *(brown)* sc in next 2 st, *(amber)* sc in next 5 st, *(brown)* sc in next 2 st, *(amber)* sc in next 23 st [48]

Rnd 10: sc in next 15 st, *(brown)* sc in next 3 st, *(amber)* sc in next 3 st *(mark the last sc with a stitch marker)*, sc in next 2 st, *(brown)* sc in next 3 st, *(amber)* sc in next 22 st [48] 3

The stitch marker on round 10 marks the top of the head.

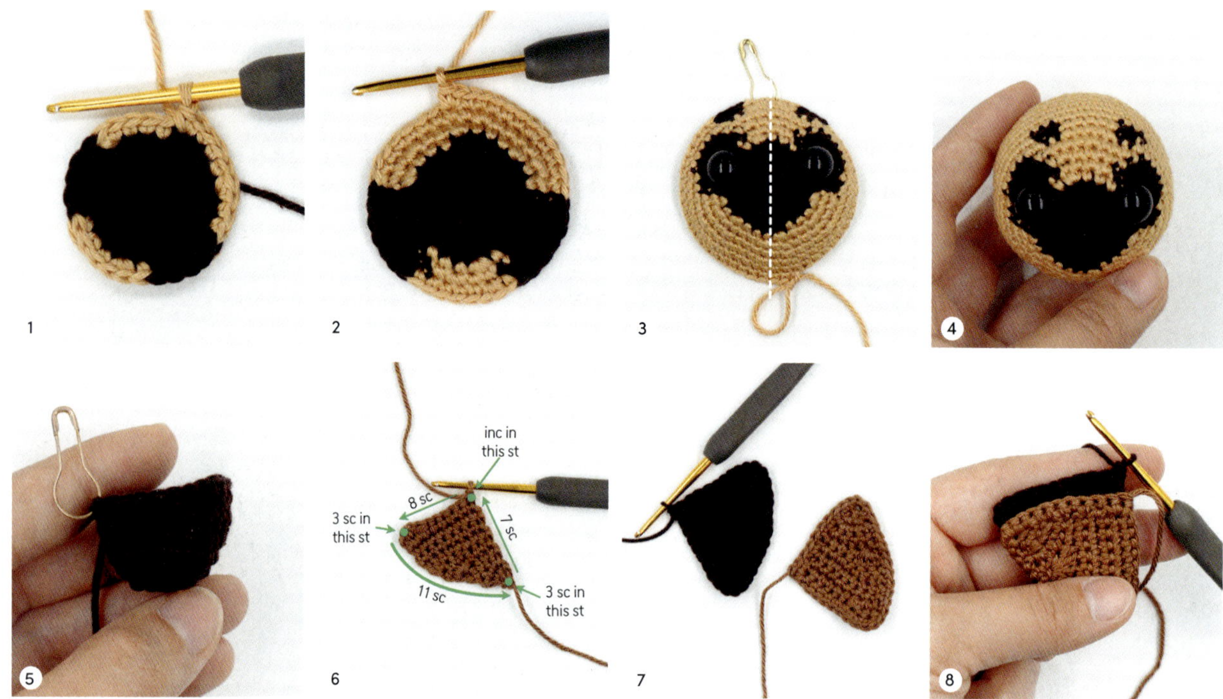

Insert the safety eyes between rounds 5-6, on the brown spots of the dog's face.

Continue crocheting in amber yarn.

Rnd 11 – 16: sc in all 48 st [48]

Rnd 17: (sc in next 3 st, dec, sc in next 3 st) repeat 6 times [42]

Rnd 18: (sc in next 5 st, dec) repeat 6 times [36]

Stuff the head with fiberfill and continue stuffing as you go.

Rnd 19: (sc in next 2 st, dec, sc in next 2 st) repeat 6 times [30]

Rnd 20: (sc in next 3 st, dec) repeat 6 times [24]

Rnd 21: (sc in next st, dec, sc in next st) repeat 6 times [18]

Rnd 22: (sc in next st, dec) repeat 6 times [12]

Rnd 23: dec 6 times [6]

Fasten off, leaving a yarn tail. Using a yarn needle, weave the yarn tail through the front loop of each remaining stitch and pull it tight to close. Weave in the yarn end (4).

SNOUT (in brown yarn)

Leave a starting yarn tail. Ch 5. Stitches are worked around both sides of the foundation chain.

Rnd 1: start in second ch from hook, inc in this ch, sc in next 2 ch, 4 sc in last ch. Continue on the other side of the foundation chain, sc in next 2 ch, inc in last ch [12]

Rnd 2: inc in next 2 st, sc in next 2 st, inc in next 4 st, sc in next 2 st, inc in next 2 st [20]

Rnd 3: sc in all 20 st [20]

Using a yarn needle, weave the starting yarn tail through the foundation chain to hide the stitch gaps.

Rnd 4: (inc in next st, sc in next 4 st) repeat 4 times [24]

Rnd 5: sc in next 2 st, hdc in next st, hdc inc in next st, hdc in next 6 st, hdc inc in next st, hdc in next st, sc in next 12 st [26]

Rnd 6: sc in next 3 st, hdc in next 10 st, sc in next 13 st [26]

Rnd 7: sc in next 4 st, hdc in next 8 st, sc in next 10 st *(mark the last sc with a stitch marker)*, sc in next 4 st [26]

Rnd 8: sc in next 3 st [3] Leave the remaining stitches unworked.

Fasten off, leaving a yarn tail for sewing. Stuff the snout with fiberfill (5).

EYELID (make 2, in brown yarn)
Ch 5. Fasten off and leave a yarn tail for sewing.

RIGHT EAR

Inner part (in light brown yarn)
Ch 2. Crochet in rows.
Row 1: start in second ch from hook, inc in this ch, ch 1, turn [2]
Row 2: sc in next st, inc in next st, ch 1, turn [3]
Row 3: sc in next 2 st, inc in next st, ch 1, turn [4]
Row 4: sc in next 2 st, hdc in next st, dc inc in next st, ch 2, turn [5]
Row 5: 3 dc in first st, hdc in next st, sc in next 3 st, ch 1, turn [7]
Row 6: sc in next 5 st, hdc in next st, dc inc in next st, ch 1, turn [8]
Row 7: sc in all 8 st, ch 1, turn [8]
Row 8: sc in all 8 st, ch 2, turn [8]
Row 9: dc in first st, hdc inc in next st, sc in next 6 st [9]
Next, we crochet around the ear 6.
Row 10: ch 1, turn, sc in next 8 st, 3 sc in next st, continue in the row-ends on the longer side of the ear, sc in next 11 st, 3 sc in next st, continue in the row-ends on the shorter side of the ear, sc in next 7 st, inc in next st [34]
Fasten off and set aside.

Outer part (in brown yarn)
Ch 2. Crochet in rows.
Row 1 – 10: repeat the instructions for the inner part, but don't fasten off.
In the next row, we'll join the inner and outer parts together 7.
Row 11: ch 1, turn, place the inner part on top of your work with the wrong side facing up and crochet through both layers 8 9, sc in next 25 st, ch 1, turn [25] Leave the remaining stitches unworked.

9

10

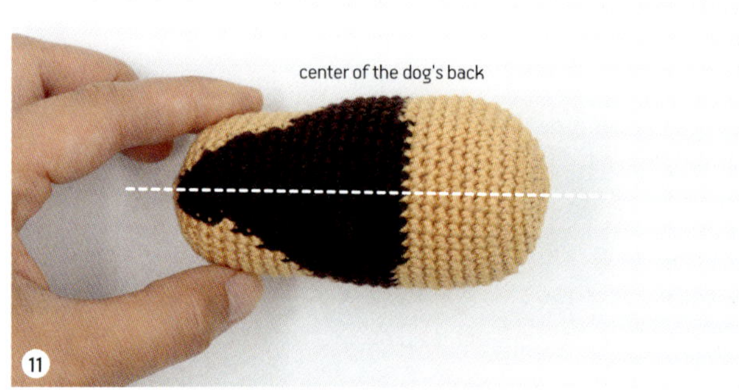

11

Row 12: sc in all 25 st [25]
Fasten off, leaving a brown yarn tail for sewing. Weave in all other yarn ends.

LEFT EAR

Inner part (in light brown yarn)

Ch 2. Crochet in rows.
Row 1: start in second ch from hook, inc in this ch, ch 1, turn [2]
Row 2: sc in next st, inc in next st, ch 1, turn [3]
Row 3: sc in next 2 st, inc in next st, ch 2, turn [4]
Row 4: dc inc in first st, hdc in next st, sc in next 2 st, ch 1, turn [5]
Row 5: sc in next 3 st, hdc in next st, 3 dc in last st, ch 2, turn [7]
Row 6: dc inc in first st, hdc in next st, sc in next 5 st, ch 1, turn [8]
Row 7 – 8: sc in all 8 st, ch 1, turn [8]
Row 9: sc in next 6 st, hdc inc in next st, dc in next st [9]
Next, we crochet around the ear.
Row 10: ch 1, turn, sc in next 8 st, 3 sc in next st, continue in the row-ends on the shorter side of the ear, sc in next 7 st, 3 sc in next st, continue in the row-ends on the longer side of the ear, sc in next 11 st, inc in next st [34]
Fasten off and set aside.

Outer part (in brown yarn)

Ch 2. Crochet in rows.
Row 1 – 10: repeat the instructions for the inner part, but don't fasten off.
In the next row, we'll join the inner and outer parts together.
Row 11: ch 1, turn, place the inner part on top of your work with the wrong side facing up and crochet through both layers, sc in next 25 st, ch 1, turn [25] Leave the remaining stitches unworked.
Row 12: sc in all 25 st [25]
Fasten off, leaving a brown yarn tail for sewing. Weave in all other yarn ends (10).

BODY (start in amber yarn)

Rnd 1: start 6 sc in a magic ring [6]
Rnd 2: inc in all 6 st [12]
Rnd 3: (sc in next st, inc in next st) repeat 6 times [18]
Rnd 4: (sc in next st, inc in next st, sc in next st) repeat 6 times [24]
Rnd 5: (sc in next 3 st, inc in next st) repeat 6 times [30]
Rnd 6: (sc in next 2 st, inc in next st, sc in next 2 st) repeat 6 times [36]
Rnd 7: (sc in next 5 st, inc in next st) repeat 6 times [42]
Rnd 8 – 14: sc in all 42 st [42]
In the next rounds, we'll alternate between amber and brown yarn. The color change is indicated in italics.
Rnd 15: sc in next 5 st, *(brown)* sc in next 11 st, *(amber)* sc in next 26 st [42]
Rnd 16: *(brown)* sc in next 21 st, *(amber)* sc in next 19 st, *(brown)* sc in next 2 st [42]
Rnd 17 – 18: sc in next 23 st, *(amber)* sc in next 17 st, *(brown)* sc in next 2 st [42]

Rnd 19: sc in next 23 st, *(amber)* sc in next 19 st [42]
Rnd 20: *(brown)* sc in next 21 st, *(amber)* sc in next 21 st [42]
Rnd 21: sc in next st, *(brown)* sc in next 19 st, *(amber)* sc in next 22 st [42]
Sc in next st. This is the new start of the round.
Rnd 22: sc in next st, *(brown)* sc in next 19 st, *(amber)* sc in next st, (sc in next 5 st, dec) repeat 3 times [39]
Rnd 23: sc in next 3 st, *(brown)* sc in next 15 st, *(amber)* sc in next 3 st, (sc in next 2 st, dec, sc in next 2 st) repeat 3 times [36]
Rnd 24: sc in next 4 st, *(brown)* sc in next 13 st, *(amber)* sc in next 4 st, hdc in next 15 st [36]
Sc in next st. This is the new start of the round.
Rnd 25 – 26: sc in next 5 st, *(brown)* sc in next 10 st, *(amber)* sc in next 21 st [36]
Rnd 27 – 28: sc in next 6 st, *(brown)* sc in next 8 st, *(amber)* sc in next 22 st [36]

Rnd 29: sc in next 7 st, *(brown)* sc in next 6 st, *(amber)* sc in next 23 st [36]
Sc in next st. This is the new start of the round.
Rnd 30 – 31: sc in next 7 st, *(brown)* sc in next 6 st, *(amber)* sc in next 23 st [36]
Rnd 32: sc in next 2 st, dec, sc in next 4 st, *(brown)* dec, sc in next 3 st, *(amber)* sc in next st, dec, sc in next 2 st, (sc in next 2 st, dec, sc in next 2 st) repeat 3 times [30]
Rnd 33: sc in next 3 st, dec, sc in next 2 st, *(brown)* sc in next st, dec, sc in next st, *(amber)* sc in next 2 st, dec, (sc in next 3 st, dec) repeat 3 times [24]
Rnd 34: sc in next st, dec, sc in next 3 st, *(brown)* dec, sc in next st, *(amber)* dec, sc in next st, (sc in next st, dec, sc in next st) repeat 3 times [18]
Continue crocheting in amber yarn.
Rnd 35: (sc in next st, dec) repeat 6 times [12]
Rnd 36: dec 6 times [6]
Fasten off, leaving a yarn tail. Using a yarn needle, weave the yarn tail through the front loop of each remaining stitch and pull it tight to close. Weave in the yarn end ⑪.

HIND LEG (make 2)

Upper part (in amber yarn)

Rnd 1: start 7 sc in a magic ring [7]
Rnd 2: inc in all 7 st [14]
Rnd 3: (sc in next st, inc in next st) repeat 7 times [21]
Rnd 4: (sc in next st, inc in next st, sc in next st) repeat 7 times [28]
Rnd 5: (sc in next 3 st, inc in next st) repeat 7 times [35]
Rnd 6: (sc in next 2 st, inc in next st, sc in next 2 st) repeat 7 times [42]
Rnd 7: sc in all 42 st [42]
Rnd 8: (sc in next 2 st, dec, sc in next 2 st) repeat 7 times [35]
Rnd 9: (sc in next 3 st, dec) repeat 7 times [28]
Rnd 10: (sc in next st, dec, sc in next st) repeat 7 times [21]
Stuff lightly with fiberfill. The upper part of the leg should have some volume, but also remain quite flat.
Rnd 11: (sc in next st, dec) repeat 7 times [14]
Rnd 12: dec 7 times [7]

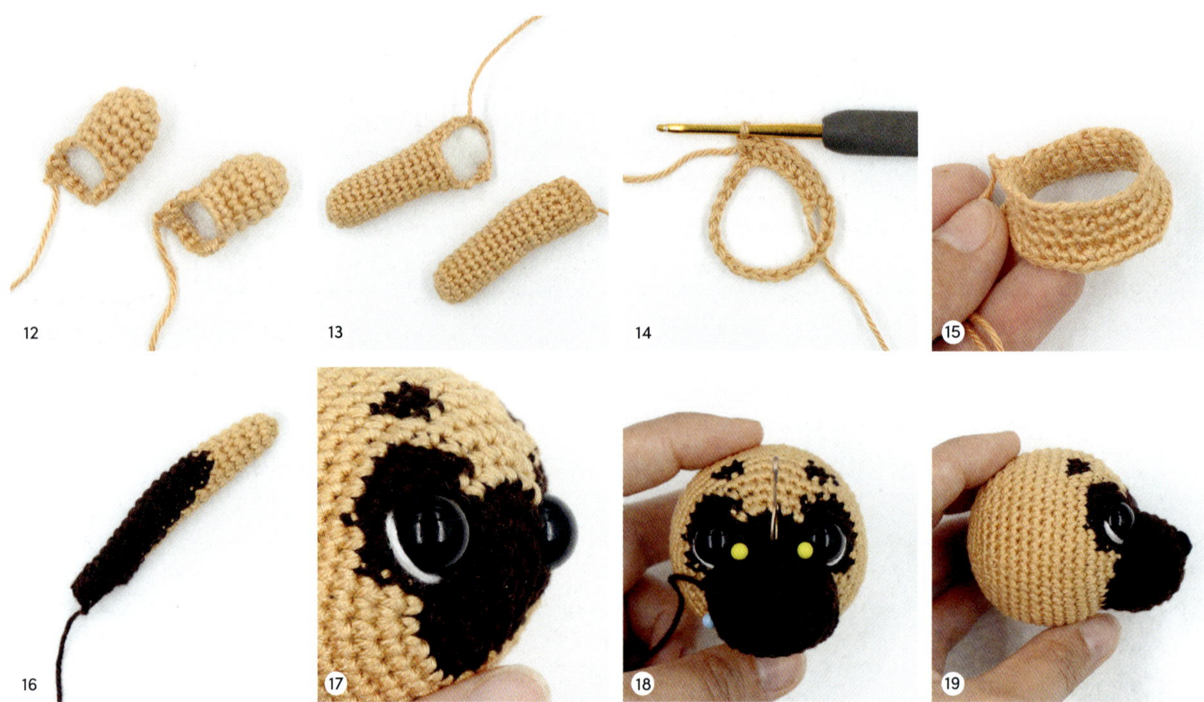

Fasten off, leaving a yarn tail. Using a yarn needle, weave the yarn tail through the front loop of each remaining stitch and pull it tight to close. Leave a yarn tail for sewing.

Foot (in amber yarn)
Rnd 1: start 6 sc in a magic ring [6]
Rnd 2: inc in all 6 st [12]
Rnd 3 – 6: sc in all 12 st [12]
Rnd 7: sc in all 12 st, ch 1, turn [12]
Continue crocheting in rows.
Row 8: skip first sc, sc in next 7 st, ch 1, turn [7] Leave the remaining stitches unworked.
Row 9: skip first sc, sc in next 6 st [6]
Fasten off, leaving a yarn tail for sewing. Stuff the feet with fiberfill (12).

FRONT LEG (make 2, in amber yarn)
Rnd 1: start 6 sc in a magic ring [6]
Rnd 2: inc in all 6 st [12]
Rnd 3 – 11: sc in all 12 st [12]
Stuff the front leg with fiberfill and continue stuffing as you go.
Rnd 12: sc in next 11 st, inc in next st [13]
Rnd 13: sc in next 6 st, inc in next st, sc in next 6 st [14]
Rnd 14: sc in next 13 st, inc in next st [15]
Rnd 15: sc in all 15 st, ch 1, turn [15]
Continue crocheting in rows.
Row 16: skip first sc, sc in next 10 st, ch 1, turn [10] Leave the remaining stitches unworked.
Row 17: skip first sc, sc in next 9 st, ch 1, turn [9]
Row 18: skip first sc, sc in next 2 st, hdc in next st, dc inc in next st, dc in next st, hdc in next st, sc in next 2 st [9]
Fasten off, leaving a yarn tail for sewing (13).

NECK (in amber yarn)
Leave a long starting yarn tail for sewing. Ch 27.
Rnd 1: start in first ch to form a circle *(make sure the chains aren't twisted),* sc in all 27 ch [27] (14)

Rnd 2: (sc in next 7 st, dec) repeat 3 times [24]
Rnd 3: (sc in next 3 st, inc in next st) repeat 6 times [30]
Rnd 4: (sc in next 2 st, inc in next st, sc in next 2 st) repeat 6 times [36]
Sc in next 2 st. Fasten off, leaving a yarn tail for sewing ⓯.

TAIL (start in amber yarn)
Rnd 1: start 6 sc in a magic ring [6]
Rnd 2: (sc in next st, inc in next st) repeat 3 times [9]
Rnd 3: sc in all 9 st [9]
Rnd 4: sc in next 4 st, inc in next st, sc in next 4 st [10]
Rnd 5: sc in next 9 st, inc in next st [11]
Rnd 6: sc in next 5 st, inc in next st, sc in next 5 st [12]
In the next rounds, we'll alternate between amber and brown yarn. The color change is indicated in italics.
Rnd 7: sc in next 5 st, *(brown)* sc in next 2 st, *(amber)* sc in next 5 st [12]
Rnd 8: sc in next 4 st, *(brown)* sc in next 4 st, *(amber)* sc in next 4 st [12]
Rnd 9: sc in next 3 st, *(brown)* sc in next 5 st, *(amber)* sc in next 4 st [12]
Rnd 10 – 11: sc in next 3 st, *(brown)* sc in next 6 st, *(amber)* sc in next 3 st [12]
Sc in next st. This is the new start of the round.
Rnd 12 – 13: sc in next 3 st, *(brown)* sc in next 6 st, *(amber)* sc in next 3 st [12]
Rnd 14: sc in next 2 st, *(brown)* sc in next 8 st, *(amber)* sc in next 2 st [12]
Rnd 15: sc in next 2 st, *(brown)* sc in next 3 st, dec, sc in next 3 st, *(amber)* sc in next 2 st [11]
Rnd 16: sc in next 2 st, *(brown)* sc in next 7 st, *(amber)* dec [10]
Rnd 17: sc in next 2 st, *(brown)* sc in next 8 st [10]
Continue crocheting in brown yarn.
Rnd 18 – 19: sc in all 10 st [10]
Rnd 20: sc in all 10 st, ch 1, turn [10]
Continue crocheting in rows.
Row 21: skip first sc, sc in next 6 st, ch 1, turn [6] Leave the remaining stitches unworked.
Row 22: skip first sc, sc in next st, hdc in next st, dc in next st, hdc in next st, sc in next st [5]
Fasten off, leaving a yarn tail for sewing ⓰.

ASSEMBLY

Assemble the eyes

- Using several strands of white thread, embroider a line along the outer edge of each eye ⓱.
- Sew the eyelids above the safety eyes.

Attach the snout

- Position the snout just below the eyes, with the stitch marker centered between them ⓲. Pin the snout in place, remove the stitch marker and sew around using the remaining yarn tail.
- Using black thread, embroider a nose on rounds 2-3 of the top side of the snout ⓳.

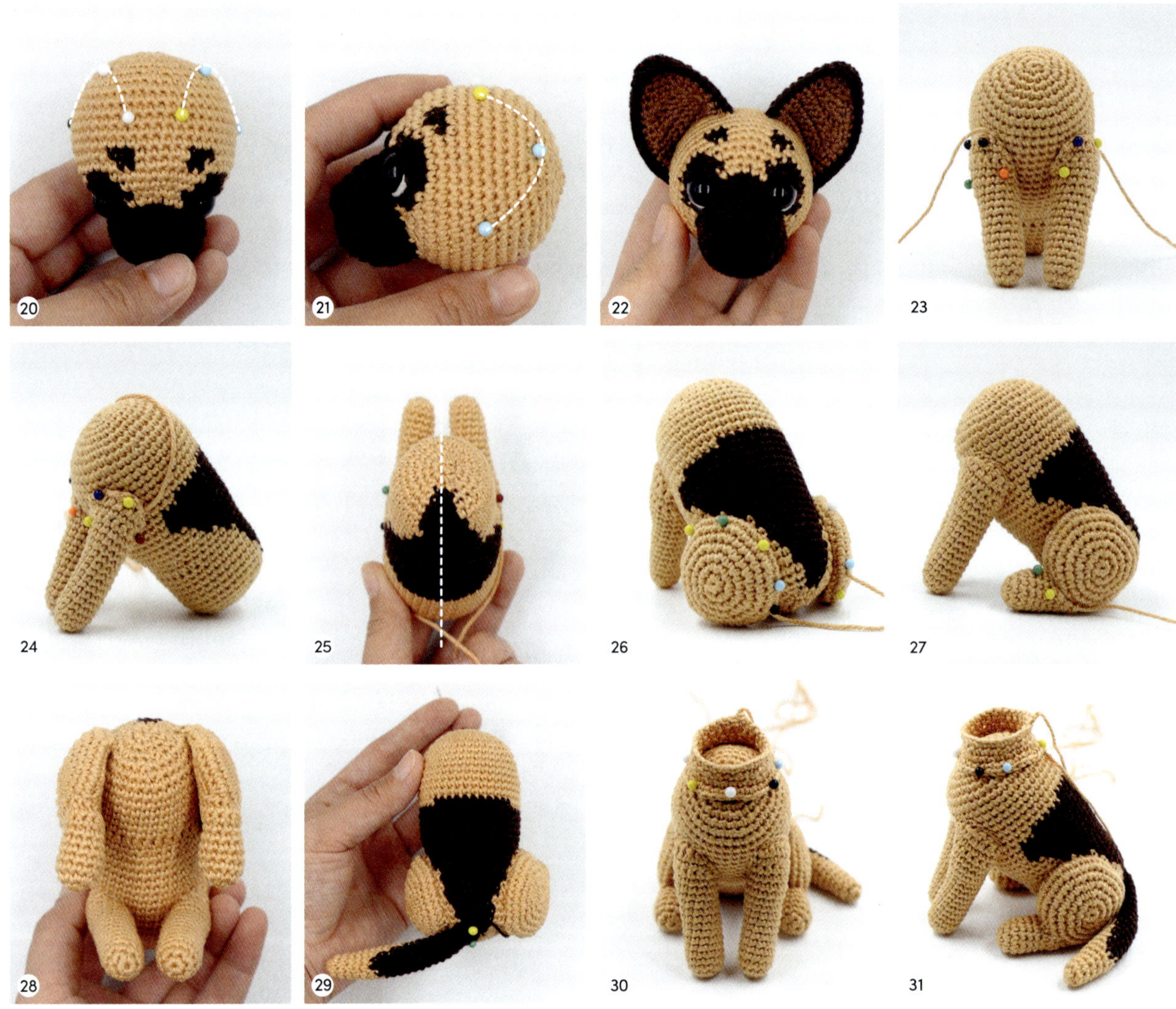

Attach the ears

- Position the ears on both sides of the head, between rounds 14-18, with an interspace of 3 stitches 20 21. Pin them in place and sew them on using the remaining yarn tails 22.

Attach the front legs

- Place the front legs on the front side of the body, on rounds 10-16. Make sure the brown patch is centered on the back of the body 23 24 25.

Attach the hind legs

- Place the upper parts of the hind legs on the lower sides of the body. It's easiest to do this while your dog is sitting on a flat surface. The upper parts should cover rounds 23-33 of the body and extend slightly toward the front. Pin them in place and sew around using the remaining yarn tails 26.
- Place the feet below the upper parts of the hind legs. The

feet should be facing the front side of the dog. Pin them in place and sew around using the remaining yarn tails 27 28.

Attach the tail

- If you want the tail to be posable, insert the wire or pipe cleaner. Otherwise, lightly stuff it with fiberfill.
- Position the tail to the back of the body, with the tail pointing to the same side you want your dog to look at. Pin it in place and sew around using the remaining yarn tail.
- Slightly bend the tail to the side 29.

Attach the neck

- Place the neck on top of the body, with round 4 at the bottom. Pin it in place and sew around using the remaining starting yarn tail 30 31.
- Stuff the neck with fiberfill.

Attach the head

- Place the head on top of the neck. Turn the head slightly to the side (in the same direction as the tail) to give your dog a cuter look. Pin it in place and sew around using the remaining yarn tail of the neck.

How to make a FOOD BOWL for your favorite cat or dog

This food bowl serves all cats & dogs in this book!

FOOD BOWL (start in gray yarn)

Rnd 1: start 6 sc in a magic ring [6]
Rnd 2: inc in all 6 st [12]
Rnd 3: (sc in next st, inc in next st) repeat 6 times [18]
Rnd 4: (sc in next st, inc in next st, sc in next st) repeat 6 times [24]
Rnd 5: (sc in next 3 st, inc in next st) repeat 6 times [30]
Rnd 6: (sc in next 2 st, inc in next st, sc in next 2 st) repeat 6 times [36]
Rnd 7 – 9: sc in all 36 st [36]
Change to red yarn.
Rnd 10: BLO slst in all 36 st [36] 32
Rnd 11: BLO sc in all 36 st [36] 33
Rnd 12: (sc in next 11 st, inc in next st) repeat 3 times [39]
Rnd 13: (sc in next 6 st, inc in next st, sc in next 6 st) repeat 3 times [42]
Rnd 14: (sc in next 13 st, inc in next st) repeat 3 times [45]
Rnd 15: sc in all 45 st [45]
Fasten off with an invisible join. Weave in the yarn ends. Place the bowl upside down on a flat surface and push the gray part down 34 35.

FOOD (in brown yarn)

Rnd 1: start 8 sc in a magic ring [8]
Fasten off with an invisible join. Weave in the yarn ends. Make as many as you need to fill the food bowl.

32

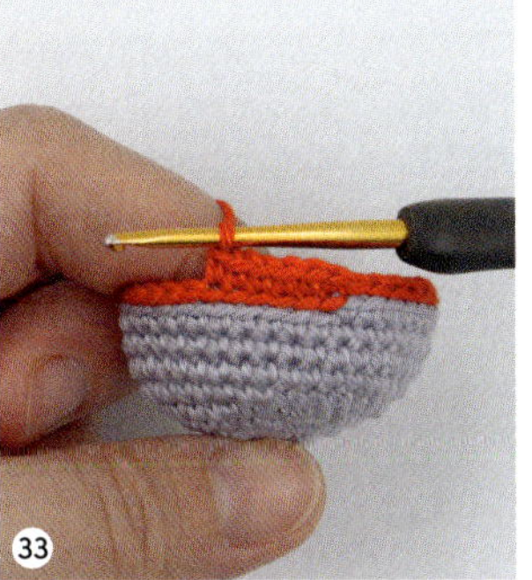
33

34

35

ENZO
the Husky

Skill level: 
Size: 4.5" / 11.5 cm tall, 4.7" / 12 cm long when made with the indicated yarn.

Amigurumi gallery: Scan or visit www.amigurumi.com/5510 to share pictures and find inspiration.

MATERIALS

• Sport weight yarn in white, gray, dark gray and pink • B-1 / 2.25 mm crochet hook • Black safety eyes (11 mm) • Black and blue embroidery thread • Yarn needle • Pins • Stitch markers • Fiberfill for stuffing • Optional: Approx. 3.1" / 8 cm of wire or pipe cleaner *(for the tail if you want it to be posable)*

HEAD (start in white yarn)

Rnd 1: start 6 sc in a magic ring [6]

Rnd 2: inc in all 6 st [12]

Rnd 3: (sc in next st, inc in next st) repeat 6 times [18]

Rnd 4: (sc in next st, inc in next st, sc in next st) repeat 6 times [24]

Change to gray yarn. In the next rounds, we'll alternate between gray and white yarn. The color change is indicated in italics.

Rnd 5: sc in next 3 st, inc in next st, *(white)* sc in next 3 st, inc in next st, *(gray)* sc in next 3 st, inc in next st, sc in next st, *(white)* sc in next 2 st, inc in next st, sc in next st, *(gray)* sc in next 2 st, inc in next st, sc in next 3 st, inc in next st [30] 1

Rnd 6: sc in next 2 st, inc in next st, sc in next 2 st, *(white)* sc in next 2 st, inc in next st, sc in next 3 st, *(gray)* sc in next st, inc in next st, sc in next 2 st, *(white)* sc in next 2 st, inc in next st, sc in next 3 st, *(gray)* sc in next st, inc in next st, sc in next 4 st, inc in next st, sc in next 2 st [36]

Rnd 7: sc in next 5 st, inc in next st, *(white)* sc in next 5 st, inc in next st, sc in next st, *(gray)* sc in next 4 st, inc in next st, *(white)* sc in next 5 st, inc in next st, sc in next st, *(gray)* sc in next 4 st, inc in next st, sc in next 5 st, inc in next st [42] 2

Rnd 8: sc in next 3 st, inc in next st, sc in next 5 st, *(white)* sc in next st, inc in next st, sc in next 3 st, *(gray)* sc in next 3 st, inc in next st, sc in next 4 st, *(white)* sc in next 2 st, inc in next st, sc in next 2 st, *(gray)* sc in next 4 st, inc in next st, sc in next 6 st, inc in next st, sc in next 3 st [48]

Continue crocheting in gray yarn.

Rnd 9 – 10: sc in all 48 st [48]

Rnd 11: sc in next 21 st *(mark the last sc with a stitch marker)*, sc in next 27 st [48]

The stitch marker on round 11 marks the top of the head. Insert the safety eyes between rounds 5-6, on the white spots of the dog's face 3.

Rnd 12 – 16: sc in all 48 st [48]
Rnd 17: (sc in next 3 st, dec, sc in next 3 st) repeat 6 times [42]
Rnd 18: (sc in next 5 st, dec) repeat 6 times [36]
Stuff the head with fiberfill and continue stuffing as you go.
Rnd 19: (sc in next 2 st, dec, sc in next 2 st) repeat 6 times [30]
Rnd 20: (sc in next 3 st, dec) repeat 6 times [24]
Rnd 21: (sc in next st, dec, sc in next st) repeat 6 times [18]
Rnd 22: (sc in next st, dec) repeat 6 times [12]
Rnd 23: dec 6 times [6]
Fasten off, leaving a yarn tail. Using a yarn needle, weave the yarn tail through the front loop of each remaining stitch and pull it tight to close. Weave in the yarn end.

SNOUT (in white yarn)

Leave a starting yarn tail. Ch 5. Stitches are worked around both sides of the foundation chain.
Rnd 1: start in second ch from hook, inc in this ch, sc in next 2 ch, 4 sc in last ch. Continue on the other side of the foundation chain, sc in next 2 ch, inc in last ch [12]
Rnd 2: inc in next 2 st, sc in next 2 st, inc in next 4 st, sc in next 2 st, inc in next 2 st [20]
Rnd 3: sc in all 20 st [20]
Using a yarn needle, weave the starting yarn tail through the foundation chain to hide the stitch gaps.
Rnd 4: (inc in next st, sc in next 4 st) repeat 4 times [24]
Rnd 5: sc in next 2 st, hdc in next st, hdc inc in next st, hdc in next 6 st, hdc inc in next st, hdc in next st, sc in next 12 st [26]
Rnd 6: sc in next 3 st, hdc in next 10 st, sc in next 13 st [26]
Rnd 7: sc in next 4 st, hdc in next 8 st, sc in next 10 st *(mark the last sc with a stitch marker)*, sc in next 4 st [26]
Rnd 8: sc in next 3 st [3] Leave the remaining stitches unworked.
Fasten off, leaving a yarn tail for sewing. Stuff the snout with fiberfill ④.

RIGHT EAR

Inner part (in pink yarn)

Ch 2. Crochet in rows.

Row 1: start in second ch from hook, inc in this ch, ch 1, turn [2]
Row 2: sc in next st, inc in next st, ch 1, turn [3]
Row 3: sc in next 2 st, inc in next st, ch 2, turn [4]
Row 4: dc inc in next st, hdc in next st, sc in next 2 st, ch 1, turn [5]
Row 5: sc in next 2 st, hdc in next st, dc in next st, dc inc in next st, ch 2, turn [6]
Row 6: dc inc in next st, dc in next st, hdc inc in next st, sc in next 3 st [8]
Next, we crochet around the ear 5.
Row 7: ch 1, turn, sc in next 7 st, 3 sc in next st, continue in the row-ends on the longer side of the ear, sc in next 8 st, 3 sc in next st, continue in the row-ends on the shorter side of the ear, sc in next 5 st, inc in next st [28]
Fasten off and set aside.

Outer part (start in gray yarn)
Ch 2. Crochet in rows.
Row 1 – 7: repeat the instructions for the inner part, but don't fasten off.
In the next row, we'll join the inner and outer parts together.
Row 8: ch 1, turn, place the inner part on top of your work with the wrong side facing up and crochet through both layers 6 7, sc in next 20 st, ch 1, turn [20] Leave the remaining stitches unworked.
Change to dark gray yarn. Leave a long gray yarn tail for sewing.
Row 9: sc in all 20 st [20]
Fasten off, leaving a dark gray yarn tail for sewing.

LEFT EAR

Inner part (in pink yarn)
Ch 2. Crochet in rows.
Row 1: start in second ch from hook, inc in this ch, ch 1, turn [2]
Row 2: sc in next st, inc in next st, ch 1, turn [3]
Row 3: sc in next 2 st, inc in next st, ch 1, turn [4]
Row 4: sc in next 2 st, hdc in next st, dc inc in next st, ch 2, turn [5]
Row 5: dc inc in next st, dc in next st, hdc in next st, sc in next 2 st, ch 1, turn [6]
Row 6: sc in next 3 st, hdc inc in next st, dc in next st, dc inc in next st [8]
Next, we crochet around the ear.

9

10

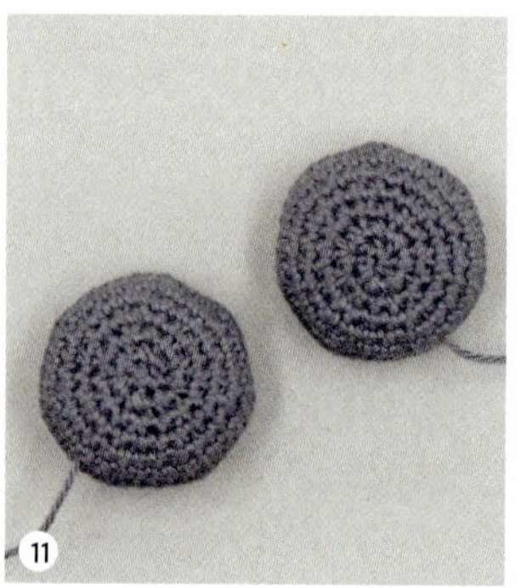
11

12

Row 7: ch 1, turn, sc in next 7 st, 3 sc in next st, continue in the row-ends on the shorter side of the ear, sc in next 5 st, 3 sc in next st, continue in the row-ends on the longer side of the ear, sc in next 8 st, inc in next st [28]
Fasten off and set aside.

Outer part (start in gray yarn)
Ch 2. Crochet in rows.
Row 1 – 7: repeat the instructions for the inner part, but don't fasten off.
In the next row, we'll join the inner and outer parts together.
Row 8: ch 1, turn, place the inner part on top of your work with the wrong side facing up and crochet through both layers, sc in next 20 st, ch 1, turn [20] Leave the remaining stitches unworked.
Change to dark gray yarn. Leave a long gray yarn tail for sewing.
Row 9: sc in all 20 st [20]
Fasten off, leaving a dark gray yarn tail for sewing 8.

BODY (start in white yarn)
Rnd 1: start 6 sc in a magic ring [6]
Rnd 2: inc in all 6 st [12]
Rnd 3: (sc in next st, inc in next st) repeat 6 times [18]
Rnd 4: (sc in next st, inc in next st, sc in next st) repeat 6 times [24]
Rnd 5: (sc in next 3 st, inc in next st) repeat 6 times [30]
In the next rounds, we'll alternate between white and gray yarn. The color change is indicated in italics.
Rnd 6: sc in next 2 st, inc in next st, sc in next 4 st, inc in next st, *(gray)* (sc in next 4 st, inc in next st) repeat 2 times, sc in next 4 st, *(white)* inc in next st, sc in next 4 st, inc in next st, sc in next 2 st [36]
Rnd 7: (sc in next 5 st, inc in next st) repeat 2 times, *(gray)* (sc in next 5 st, in in next st) repeat 2 times, *(white)* (sc in next 5 st, inc in next st) repeat 2 times [42]
Rnd 8: sc in next 10 st, *(gray)* sc in next 22 st, *(white)* sc in next 10 st [42]
Rnd 9: sc in next 9 st, *(gray)* sc in next 24 st, *(white)* sc in next 9 st [42]
Rnd 10: sc in next 7 st, *(gray)* sc in next 28 st, *(white)* sc in next 7 st [42]
Rnd 11: sc in next 6 st, *(gray)* sc in next 30 st, *(white)* sc in next 6 st [42]
Sc in next st. This is the new start of the round.
Rnd 12 – 13: sc in next 4 st, *(gray)* sc in next 34 st, *(white)* sc in next 4 st [42]
Rnd 14 – 15: sc in next 5 st, *(gray)* sc in next 32 st, *(white)* sc in next 5 st [42]
Rnd 16: sc in next 6 st, *(gray)* sc in next 30 st, *(white)* sc in next 6 st [42]
Rnd 17: sc in next 5 st, *(gray)* sc in next 32 st, *(white)* sc in next 5 st [42]
Sc in next st. This is the new start of the round.
Stuff the body with fiberfill and continue stuffing as you go.
Rnd 18: sc in next 5 st, *(gray)* sc in next 32 st, *(white)* sc in next 5 st [42] 9
Rnd 19: sc in next 7 st, *(gray)* sc in next 28 st, *(white)* sc in next 7 st [42]

Rnd 20: sc in next 8 st, *(gray)* sc in next 26 st, *(white)* sc in next 8 st [42]
Rnd 21: sc in next 9 st, *(gray)* sc in next 24 st, *(white)* sc in next 9 st [42]
Rnd 22: dec, sc in next 5 st, dec, sc in next st, *(gray)* sc in next 22 st, *(white)* sc in next 3 st, dec, sc in next 5 st [39]
Rnd 23: dec, sc in next 4 st, dec, sc in next 2 st, *(gray)* sc in next 20 st, *(white)* sc in next 3 st, dec, sc in next 4 st [36]
Rnd 24: sc in next 8 st, *(gray)* sc in next 20 st, *(white)* sc in next st, hdc in next 7 st [36]
Rnd 25: hdc in next 7 st, sc in next st, *(gray)* sc in next 20 st, *(white)* sc in next 8 st [36]
Rnd 26: sc in next 7 st, *(gray)* sc in next 23 st, *(white)* sc in next 6 st [36]
Rnd 27: sc in next 6 st, *(gray)* sc in next 25 st, *(white)* sc in next 5 st [36]
Rnd 28: sc in next 5 st, *(gray)* sc in next 27 st, *(white)* sc in next 4 st [36]
Rnd 29: sc in next 5 st, *(gray)* sc in next 28 st, *(white)* sc in next 3 st [36]
Rnd 30: sc in next 4 st, *(gray)* sc in next 30 st, *(white)* sc in next 2 st [36]
Rnd 31: sc in next 4 st, *(gray)* sc in next 31 st, *(white)* sc in next st [36]
Rnd 32: sc in next 2 st, *(gray)* dec, sc in next 2 st, (sc in next 2 st, dec, sc in next 2 st) repeat 5 times [30]
Continue crocheting in gray yarn.
Rnd 33: (sc in next 3 st, dec) repeat 6 times [24]
Rnd 34: (sc in next st, dec, sc in next st) repeat 6 times [18]
Rnd 35: (sc in next st, dec) repeat 6 times [12]
Rnd 36: dec 6 times [6]
Fasten off, leaving a yarn tail. Using a yarn needle, weave the yarn tail through the front loop of each remaining stitch and pull it tight to close. Weave in the yarn end ⑩.

HIND LEG (make 2)

Upper part (in gray yarn)

Rnd 1: start 7 sc in a magic ring [7]
Rnd 2: inc in all 7 st [14]
Rnd 3: (sc in next st, inc in next st) repeat 7 times [21]
Rnd 4: (sc in next st, inc in next st, sc in next st) repeat 7 times [28]
Rnd 5: (sc in next 3 st, inc in next st) repeat 7 times [35]
Rnd 6: (sc in next 2 st, inc in next st, sc in next 2 st) repeat 7 times [42]
Rnd 7: sc in all 42 st [42]
Rnd 8: (sc in next 2 st, dec, sc in next 2 st) repeat 7 times [35]
Rnd 9: (sc in next 3 st, dec) repeat 7 times [28]
Rnd 10: (sc in next st, dec, sc in next st) repeat 7 times [21]
Stuff lightly with fiberfill. The upper part of the leg should have some volume, but also remain quite flat.
Rnd 11: (sc in next st, dec) repeat 7 times [14]
Rnd 12: dec 7 times [7]
Fasten off, leaving a yarn tail. Using a yarn needle, weave the yarn tail through the front loop of each remaining stitch and pull it tight to close. Bring the yarn tail out on the side of the upper part, between rounds 6-7 ⑪.

Hind foot (start in white yarn)

Rnd 1: start 6 sc in a magic ring [6]
Rnd 2: inc in all 6 st [12]
Rnd 3 – 6: sc in all 12 st [12]
Change to gray yarn.
Rnd 7: sc in all 12 st [12]
Rnd 8: sc in next 5 st, ch 1, turn [5] Leave the remaining stitches unworked.
Continue crocheting in rows.
Row 9: skip first sc, sc in next 8 st, ch 1, turn [8] Leave the remaining stitches unworked.
Row 10: skip first sc, sc in next 7 st, ch 1, turn [7]
Row 11: skip first sc, sc in next 6 st, ch 1, turn [6]
Row 12: skip first sc, sc in next 5 st [5]
Fasten off, leaving a yarn tail for sewing. Stuff the hind feet with fiberfill ⑫.

FRONT LEG (make 2)

Upper part (in gray yarn)

Rnd 1: start 7 sc in a magic ring [7]

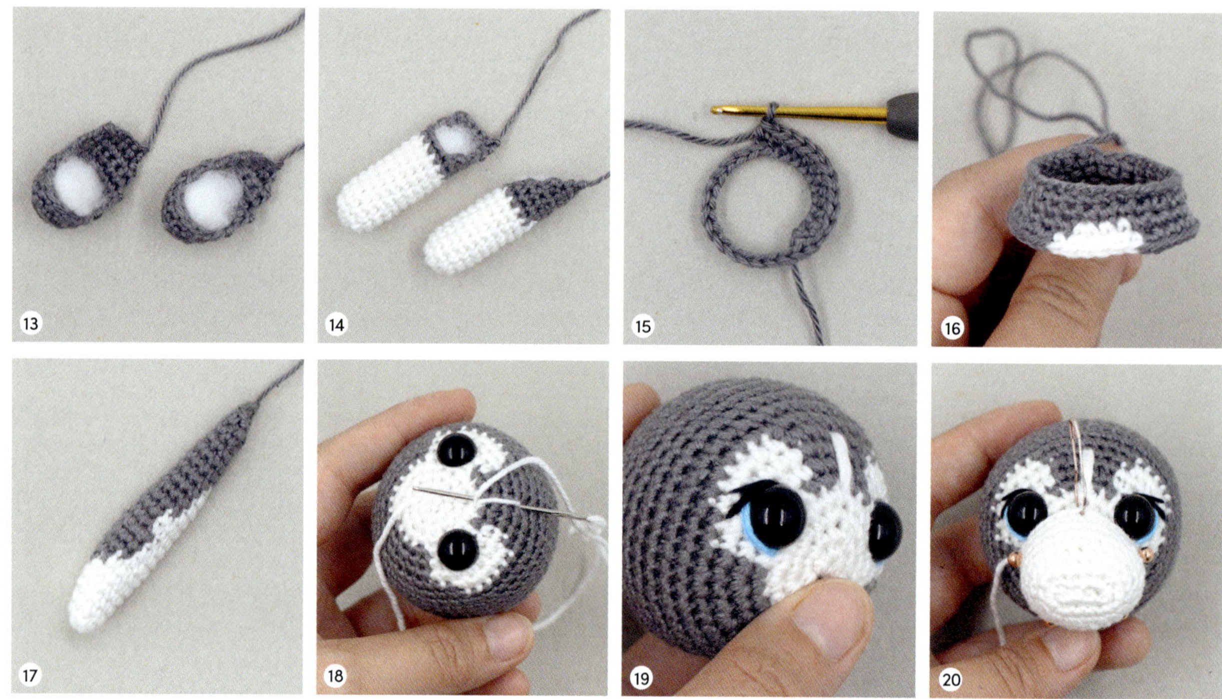

Rnd 2: inc in all 7 st [14]
Rnd 3: sc in all 14 st [14]
Rnd 4: sc in all 14 st, ch 1, turn [14]
Continue crocheting in rows.
Row 5: skip first sc, sc in next 9 st, ch 1, turn [9] Leave the remaining stitches unworked.
Row 6: skip first sc, sc in next 8 st, ch 1, turn [8]
Row 7: skip first sc, sc in next 7 st, ch 1, turn [7]
Row 8: skip first sc, sc in next 6 st, ch 1, turn [6]
Row 9: skip first sc, sc in next 5 st, ch 1, turn [5]
Row 10: skip first sc, sc in next 4 st [4]
Fasten off, leaving a yarn tail for sewing. Stuff the upper part with fiberfill (13).

Front foot (start in white yarn)
Rnd 1: start 6 sc in a magic ring [6]
Rnd 2: inc in all 6 st [12]
Rnd 3 – 11: sc in all 12 st [12]
Change to gray yarn.
Rnd 12: sc in all 12 st [12]
Rnd 13: sc in next 5 st, ch 1, turn [5] Leave the remaining stitches unworked.
Continue crocheting in rows.
Row 14: skip first sc, sc in next 8 st, ch 1, turn [8] Leave the remaining stitches unworked.
Row 15: skip first sc, sc in next 7 st, ch 1, turn [7]
Row 16: skip first sc, sc in next 6 st, ch 1, turn [6]
Row 17: skip first sc, sc in next 5 st [5]
Fasten off, leaving a yarn tail for sewing. Stuff the front feet with fiberfill (14).

NECK (start in gray yarn)
Leave a long starting yarn tail for sewing. Ch 27.
Rnd 1: start in first ch to form a circle *(make sure the chains aren't twisted)*, sc in all 27 ch [27] (15)
Rnd 2: (sc in next 7 st, dec) repeat 3 times [24]
In the next rounds, we'll alternate between gray and white yarn. The color change is indicated in italics.

Rnd 3: (sc in next 3 st, inc in next st) repeat 2 times, sc in next 3 st, *(white)* inc in next st, sc in next 2 st, *(gray)* sc in next st, inc in next st, (sc in next 3 st, inc in next st) repeat 2 times [30]
Rnd 4: (sc in next 2 st, inc in next st, sc in next 2 st) repeat 2 times, sc in next st, inc in next st, *(white)* sc in next 6 st, *(gray)* inc in next st, sc in next st, (sc in next 2 st, inc in next st, sc in next 2 st) repeat 2 times [36]
Sc in next 2 st. Fasten off, leaving a yarn tail for sewing 16.

TAIL (start in white yarn)
Rnd 1: start 6 sc in a magic ring [6]
Rnd 2: (sc in next st, inc in next st) repeat 3 times [9]
Rnd 3: sc in all 9 st [9]
Rnd 4: sc in next 4 st, inc in next st, sc in next 4 st [10]
Rnd 5: sc in next 9 st, inc in next st [11]
Rnd 6: sc in next 5 st, inc in next st, sc in next 5 st [12]
In the next rounds, we'll alternate between white and gray yarn. The color change is indicated in italics.
Rnd 7: sc in next 5 st, *(gray)* sc in next 2 st, *(white)* sc in next 5 st [12]
Rnd 8: sc in next 4 st, *(gray)* sc in next 4 st, *(white)* sc in next 4 st [12]
Rnd 9: sc in next 3 st, *(gray)* sc in next 5 st, *(white)* sc in next 4 st [12]
Rnd 10 – 11: sc in next 3 st, *(gray)* sc in next 6 st, *(white)* sc in next 3 st [12]
Sc in next st. This is the new start of the round.
Rnd 12 – 13: sc in next 3 st, *(gray)* sc in next 6 st, *(white)* sc in next 3 st [12]
Rnd 14: sc in next 2 st, *(gray)* sc in next 8 st, *(white)* sc in next 2 st [12]
Rnd 15: sc in next 2 st, *(gray)* sc in next 3 st, dec, sc in next 3 st, *(white)* sc in next 2 st [11]
Rnd 16: sc in next 2 st, *(gray)* sc in next 7 st, *(white)* dec [10]
Rnd 17: sc in next 2 st, *(gray)* sc in next 8 st [10]
Continue crocheting in gray yarn.
Rnd 18 – 19: sc in all 10 st [10]
Rnd 20: sc in all 10 st, ch 1, turn [10]
Continue crocheting in rows.
Row 21: skip first sc, sc in next 6 st, ch 1, turn [6] Leave the remaining stitches unworked.
Row 22: skip first sc, sc in next st, hdc in next st, dc in next st, hdc in next st, sc in next st [5]
Fasten off, leaving a yarn tail for sewing 17.

ASSEMBLY

Add the details on the face

- Using white yarn embroider a stripe on the dog's forehead. It should cover 4 gray rounds and should be centered between the white patches around the eyes 18.
- Using several strands of blue thread, embroider a line along the outer edge of each eye.
- Using black thread, embroider the eyelashes above the eyes 19.

Attach the snout

- Position the snout just below the eyes, with the stitch marker

centered between them 20. Pin it in place, remove the stitch marker and sew around using the remaining yarn tail.

- Using black thread, embroider a nose on rounds 2-3 of the top side of the snout 21.

Attach the ears

- Position the ears on both sides of the head, between rounds 14-18, with an interspace of 3 stitches 22 23. Pin them in place and sew them on using the remaining yarn tails 24.

Attach the front legs

- Place the upper parts on the front sides of the body, on rounds 9-15. Make sure the white patch is centered on the bottom of the body.
- Pin them in place and check to see if the puppy can sit properly. Adjust the position if needed and sew around using the remaining yarn tails 25 26 27.
- Place the front feet under the upper parts, pointing to the front side of the body. Pin them in place and sew around

using the remaining yarn tails 28.

Attach the hind legs

- Place the upper parts of the hind legs on the back sides of the body. It's easiest to do this while your dog is lying on a flat surface. The upper parts should cover rounds 21-32 of the body. Pin them in place and sew around using the remaining yarn tails 29.
- Place the hind feet below the upper parts of the hind legs. The feet should be facing the front side of the dog. Pin them in place and sew around using the remaining yarn tails 30.

Attach the tail

- If you want the tail to be posable, insert the wire or pipe cleaner. Otherwise, lightly stuff it with fiberfill.
- Position the tail to the back of the body, with the tail pointing to the same side you want your dog to look at. Make sure the white patch is turned toward the body. Pin it in place and sew around using the remaining yarn tail.
- Slightly bend the tail to the side 31.

Attach the neck

- Position round 4 of the neck on top of the body with the white patch aligned with the dog's white chest. Pin it in place and sew around using the remaining yarn tail 32.

Attach the head

- Place the head on top of the neck. Turn the head slightly to the side (in the same direction as the tail) to give your dog a cuter look. Pin it in place and sew around using the remaining yarn tail.

LEXI
the Labrador Retriever

Skill level: ● ○ ○
Size: 5.1" / 13 cm tall (sitting) or 4.3" / 11 cm tall (lying down) when made with the indicated yarn.

Amigurumi gallery: Scan or visit www.amigurumi.com/5511 to share pictures and find inspiration.

MATERIALS

• Sport weight yarn in beige • B-1 / 2.25 mm crochet hook • Safety eyes (8 mm)
• Black and white embroidery thread • Yarn needle • Pins • Stitch markers • Fiberfill for stuffing
• Optional: Approx. 3.2" / 8 cm of wire or pipe cleaner *(for the tail if you want it to be posable)*

Follow the main instructions to make the sitting Labrador. If you would like to make the lying dog instead, be sure to read the additional instructions on page 103 first.

HEAD (in beige yarn)
Rnd 1: start 6 sc in a magic ring [6]
Rnd 2: inc in all 6 st [12]
Rnd 3: (sc in next st, inc in next st) repeat 6 times [18]
Rnd 4: (sc in next st, inc in next st, sc in next st) repeat 6 times [24]
Rnd 5: (sc in next 3 st, inc in next st) repeat 6 times [30]
Rnd 6: (sc in next 2 st, inc in next st, sc in next 2 st) repeat 6 times [36]
Rnd 7: (sc in next 5 st, inc in next st) repeat 6 times [42]
Rnd 8: (sc in next 3 st, inc in next st, sc in next 3 st) repeat 6 times [48]
Rnd 9 – 18: sc in all 48 st [48]
Rnd 19: (sc in next 3 st, dec, sc in next 3 st) repeat 6 times [42]
Insert the safety eyes between rounds 14 and 15, with an interspace of 8 stitches. Stuff the head with fiberfill and continue stuffing as you go.
Rnd 20: (sc in next 5 st, dec) repeat 6 times [36]
Rnd 21: (sc in next 2 st, dec, sc in next 2 st) repeat 6 times [30]
Rnd 22: (sc in next 4 st, dec, sc in next 4 st) repeat 3 times [27]
Rnd 23 – 24: sc in all 27 st [27]
Rnd 25: (sc in next 4 st, inc in next st, sc in next 4 st) repeat 3 times [30]
Rnd 26: (sc in next 2 st, inc in next st, sc in next 2 st) repeat 6 times [36]
Fasten off, leaving a yarn tail for sewing .

SNOUT (in beige yarn)
For the snout, follow the same pattern as the German Shepherd on page 80 ②.

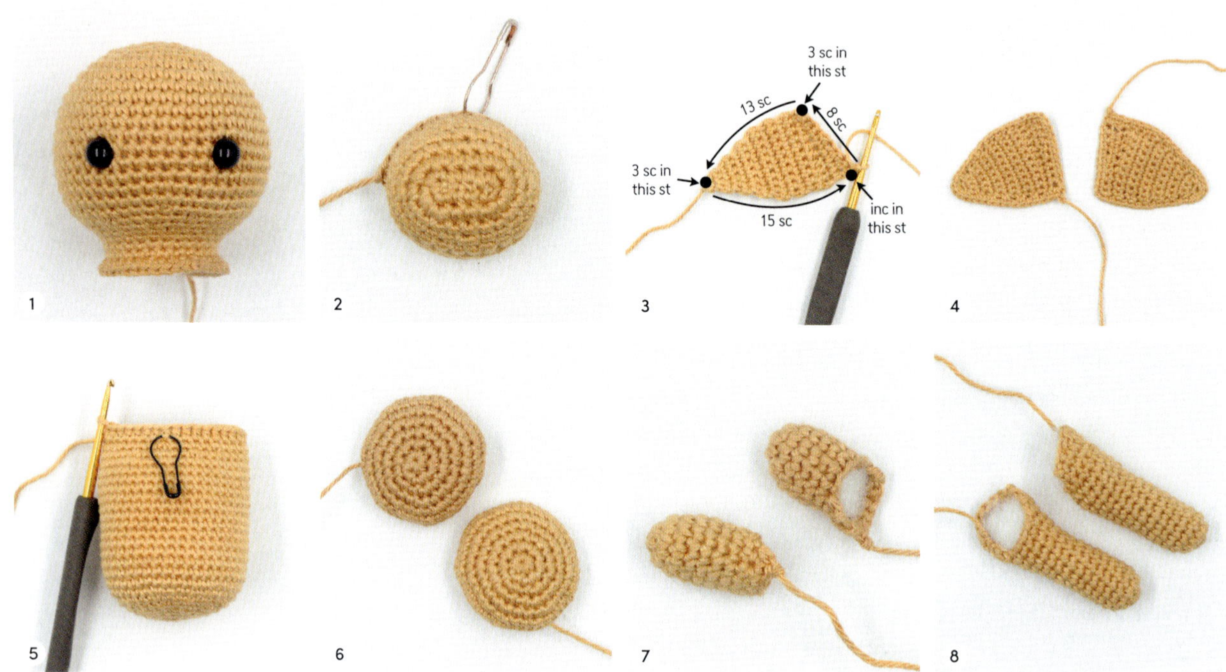

1 2 3 4 5 6 7 8

RIGHT EAR (in beige yarn)

Ch 2. Crochet in rows.

Row 1: start in second ch from hook, inc in this ch, ch 1, turn [2]

Row 2: sc in next st, inc in next st, ch 1, turn [3]

Row 3: sc in next 2 st, inc in next st, ch 1, turn [4]

Row 4: sc in next 3 st, inc in next st, ch 1, turn [5]

Row 5: sc in next 4 st, inc in next st, ch 1, turn [6]

Row 6: sc in next 5 st, inc in next st, ch 1, turn [7]

Row 7: sc in next 6 st, inc in next st, ch 1, turn [8]

Row 8: sc in next 7 st, inc in next st, ch 1, turn [9]

Row 9 – 11: sc in all 9 st, ch 1, turn [9]

Row 12: sc in all 9 st, ch 2, turn [9]

Row 13: dc in next 3 st, hdc in next 3 st, sc in next 3 st, ch 1, turn [9]

Row 14: sc in next 4 st, hdc in next 2 st, dc in next 3 st [9]

Next, we crochet around the ear 3.

Row 15: ch 1, turn, sc in next 8 st, 3 sc in next st, continue in the row-ends on the shorter side of the ear, sc in next 13 st, 3 sc in next st, continue in the row-ends on the longer side of the ear, sc in next 15 st, inc in next st [44]

Fasten off, leaving a yarn tail for sewing.

LEFT EAR (in beige yarn)

Ch 2. Crochet in rows.

Row 1 – 11: repeat the instructions for the right ear.

Row 12: sc in all 9 st, ch 1, turn [9]

Row 13: sc in next 3 st, hdc in next 3 st, dc in next 3 st, ch 2, turn [9]

Row 14: dc in next 3 st, hdc in next 2 st, sc in next 4 st [9]

Next, we crochet around the ear.

Row 15: ch 1, turn, sc in next 8 st, 3 sc in next st, continue in the row-ends on the longer side of the ear, sc in next 15 st, 3 sc in next st, continue in the row-ends on the shorter side of the ear, sc in next 13 st, inc in next st [44]

Fasten off, leaving a yarn tail for sewing 4.

BODY (in beige yarn)

Rnd 1: start 6 sc in a magic ring [6]

Rnd 2: inc in all 6 st [12]
Rnd 3: (sc in next st, inc in next st) repeat 6 times [18]
Rnd 4: (sc in next st, inc in next st, sc in next st) repeat 6 times [24]
Rnd 5: (sc in next 3 st, inc in next st) repeat 6 times [30]
Rnd 6: (sc in next 2 st, inc in next st, sc in next 2 st) repeat 6 times [36]
Rnd 7: (sc in next 5 st, inc in next st) repeat 6 times [42]
Rnd 8 – 21: sc in all 42 st [42]
Rnd 22: sc in next 21 st, (sc in next 5 st, dec) repeat 3 times [39]
Rnd 23: sc in next 21 st, (sc in next 2 st, dec, sc in next 2 st) repeat 3 times [36]
Rnd 24: sc in next 21 st, hdc in next 8 st *(mark the post of the last hdc you made with a stitch marker* 5*)*, hdc in next 7 st [36]
Rnd 25 – 31: sc in all 36 st [36]
Rnd 32: (sc in next 2 st, dec, sc in next 2 st) repeat 6 times [30]
Rnd 33: (sc in next 3 st, dec) repeat 6 times [24]
Rnd 34: (sc in next st, dec, sc in next st) repeat 6 times [18]
Rnd 35: (sc in next st, dec) repeat 6 times [12]
Rnd 36: dec 6 times [6]
Fasten off, leaving a yarn tail. Using a yarn needle, weave the yarn tail through the front loop of each remaining stitch and pull it tight to close. Weave in the yarn end.

HIND LEG (make 2, in beige yarn)

For the upper part 6 and feet 7, follow the same pattern as the German Shepherd on pages 83-84.

FRONT LEG (make 2, in beige yarn)

For the front leg 8, follow the same pattern as the German Shepherd on page 84.

TAIL (in beige yarn)

Rnd 1: start 6 sc in a magic ring [6]
Rnd 2: sc in all 6 st [6]
Rnd 3: sc in next 5 st, inc in next st [7]
Rnd 4: sc in all 7 st [7]
Rnd 5: sc in next 3 st, inc in next st, sc in next 3 st [8]
Rnd 6: sc in all 8 st [8]
Rnd 7: sc in next 7 st, inc in next st [9]
Rnd 8: sc in next 4 st, inc in next st, sc in next 4 st [10]
Rnd 9 – 15: sc in all 10 st [10]
Rnd 16: sc in next 4 st, dec, sc in next 4 st [9]
Rnd 17: sc in all 9 st [9]
Rnd 18: sc in all 9 st, ch 1, turn [9]
Continue crocheting in rows.
Row 19: skip first sc, sc in next 5 st, ch 1, turn [5] Leave the remaining stitches unworked.
Row 20: skip first sc, sc in next 4 st, ch 1, turn [4]
Row 21: skip first sc, sc in next 3 st [3]
Fasten off, leaving a yarn tail for sewing.

ASSEMBLY

Assemble the eyes

- Using several strands of white thread, embroider a line along

the outer edge of each eye.

- Using black thread, embroider the upper outline 9.

Attach the snout

- Position the snout just below the eyes, with the stitch marker centered between them 10. Pin it in place, remove the stitch marker and sew around using the remaining yarn tail.
- Using black thread, embroider a nose on rounds 2-3 of the top side of the snout 11.

Attach the ears

- Position the ears on both sides of the head, between rounds 5-14, with the wrong side facing forward 12 13 14. Pin them in place and sew them on using the remaining yarn tails.
- Bend the ears down and sew them to the face to secure the position 15.

Attach the front legs

- Place the front legs on the front side of the body, covering rounds 10-16 of the body. Ensure that the stitch marker in round 24 is centered on the belly. Pin them in place and check to see if the puppy can sit properly. Adjust the position if needed and sew around using the remaining yarn tails 16.

Attach the hind legs

- Place the upper parts of the hind legs on the lower sides of the body. It's easiest to do this while your dog is sitting on a flat surface. The upper parts should cover rounds 23-33 of the body and extend slightly toward the front. Pin them in place and sew around using the remaining yarn tails.
- Place the feet below the upper parts of the hind legs. The feet should be facing the front side of the dog. Pin them in place and sew around using the remaining yarn tails 17 18.

Attach the tail

- If you want the tail to be posable, insert the wire or pipe cleaner. Otherwise, lightly stuff it with fiberfill.
- Position the tail to the back of the body, with the tail pointing to the same side you want your dog to look at. Pin it in place and sew around using the remaining yarn tail.
- Slightly bend the tail to the side 19.

Attach the head

- Place the head on top of the body. Turn the head slightly to the side (in the direction of the tail) to give your dog a cuter look. Pin it in place and sew around using the remaining yarn tail.

How to make a Labrador lying down

- Follow the pattern instructions for the Husky's front legs on pages 93-94 (make both the upper parts of the legs and the front feet). Please note that you don't need to make any color changes.
- Assemble the head by following the Labrador instructions on pages 101-103.
- Assemble the body by following the Husky instructions on pages 96-97.

JUNO
the Marmalade Cat

Skill level: ● ● ○
Size: 3.5" / 9 cm tall, 6" / 15 cm long when made with the indicated yarn.

Amigurumi gallery: Scan or visit www.amigurumi.com/5512 to share pictures and find inspiration.

MATERIALS

- Sport weight yarn in orange and amber • B-1 / 2.25 mm crochet hook • Safety eyes (11 mm)
- White sewing thread *(for the whiskers)* • Black and green embroidery thread
- Any type of yarn *(for the yarn ball)* • Yarn needle • Pins • Stitch markers
- Fiberfill for stuffing • Approx. 4" / 10 cm of wire or pipe cleaner for the tail

HEAD (start in orange yarn)

Rnd 1: start 6 sc in a magic ring [6]

Rnd 2: inc in all 6 st [12]

Rnd 3: (sc in next st, inc in next st) repeat 6 times [18]

Rnd 4: (sc in next st, inc in next st, sc in next st) repeat 6 times [24]

Rnd 5: (sc in next 3 st, inc in next st) repeat 6 times [30]

Rnd 6: (sc in next 2 st, inc in next st, sc in next 2 st) repeat 6 times [36]

Rnd 7: (sc in next 5 st, inc in next st) repeat 6 times [42]

In the next rounds, we'll alternate between orange and amber yarn. The color change is indicated in italics.

Rnd 8: (sc in next 3 st, inc in next st, sc in next 3 st) repeat 2 times, sc in next 3 st, inc in next st, sc in next st, *(amber)* sc in next 5 st, *(orange)* inc in next st, sc in next 3 st, (sc in next 3 st, inc in next st, sc in next 3 st) repeat 2 times [48]

Rnd 9: (sc in next 7 st, inc in next st) repeat 6 times [54]

Rnd 10: sc in next 26 st, *(amber)* sc in next 3 st, *(orange)* sc in next 25 st [54]

Rnd 11: sc in next 10 st, *(amber)* sc in next 7 st, *(orange)* sc in next 21 st, *(amber)* sc in next 7 st, *(orange)* sc in next 9 st [54]

Rnd 12: sc in next 26 st, *(amber)* sc in next 3 st, *(orange)* sc in next 25 st [54]

Rnd 13: sc in next 8 st, *(amber)* sc in next 11 st, *(orange)* sc in next 17 st, *(amber)* sc in next 11 st, *(orange)* sc in next 7 st [54]

Rnd 14: sc in all 54 st [54]

Rnd 15: sc in next 9 st, *(amber)* sc in next 11 st, *(orange)* sc in next 15 st, *(amber)* sc in next 11 st, *(orange)* sc in next 8 st [54]

Rnd 16: sc in all 54 st [54]

Rnd 17: sc in next 11 st, *(amber)* sc in next 8 st, *(orange)*

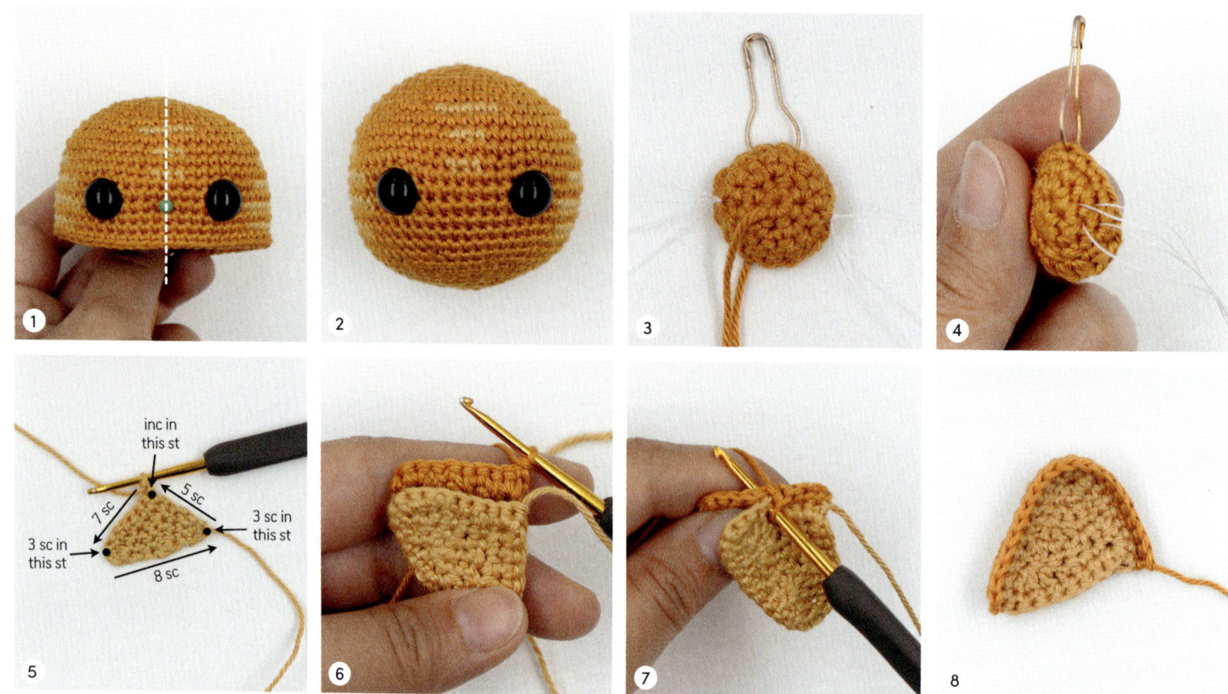

sc in next 17 st, *(amber)* sc in next 8 st, *(orange)* sc in next 10 st [54]

Continue crocheting in orange yarn.

Rnd 18: sc in all 54 st [54]

Use a safety pin or stitch marker to mark the middle of round 15 (this pin or marker should be aligned with the center of the amber stripes on rounds 8, 10 and 12 and indicates the center of the cat's face). Insert the safety eyes between rounds 14-15, with an interspace of 9 stitches ❶.

Rnd 19: (sc in next 7 st, dec) repeat 6 times [48]

Rnd 20: (sc in next 3 st, dec, sc in next 3 st) repeat 6 times [42]

Rnd 21: (sc in next 5 st, dec) repeat 6 times [36]

Stuff the head with fiberfill and continue stuffing as you go.

Rnd 22: (sc in next 2 st, dec, sc in next 2 st) repeat 6 times [30]

Rnd 23: (sc in next 3 st, dec) repeat 6 times [24]

Rnd 24: (sc in next st, dec, sc in next st) repeat 6 times [18]

Rnd 25: (sc in next st, dec) repeat 6 times [12]

Rnd 26: dec 6 times [6]

Fasten off, leaving a yarn tail. Using a yarn needle, weave the yarn tail through the front loop of each remaining stitch and pull it tight to close. Weave in the yarn end ❷.

SNOUT (in orange yarn)

Rnd 1: start 7 sc in a magic ring [7]

Rnd 2: inc in all 7 st [14]

Rnd 3: sc in next 10 st, hdc inc in next st, dc in next 3 st [15]

Rnd 4: dc in next 2 st, hdc inc in next st, sc in next 4 st *(mark the last sc with a stitch marker)*, sc in next 5 st [13] Leave the remaining stitches unworked.

Fasten off, leaving a yarn tail for sewing.

Attach the whiskers

Prepare 4 strands of white sewing thread, each about 6" / 15 cm long. Note that the stitch marker on the last round indicates the top center of the snout. With the wrong side of the snout facing you, tie 2 strands on the left and 2 strands on the right, keeping the knots on the inside so they remain hidden from the front 3. Each knot creates 2 loose ends, giving you 4 strands on each side. Pull each strand through a separate stitch gap to the front side of the snout 4.

RIGHT EAR

Inner part (in amber yarn)
Ch 2. Crochet in rows.
Row 1: start in second ch from hook, inc in this ch, ch 1, turn [2]
Row 2: sc in next st, inc in next st, ch 1, turn [3]
Row 3: sc in next 2 st, inc in next st, ch 2, turn [4]
Row 4: dc inc in next st, hdc in next st, sc in next 2 st, ch 1, turn [5]
Row 5: sc in next 2 st, hdc in next st, dc in next st, dc inc in next st, ch 2, turn [6]
Row 6: dc inc in next st, dc in next st, hdc inc in next st, sc in next 3 st [8]
Next, we crochet around the ear 5.
Row 7: ch 1, turn, sc in next 7 st, 3 sc in next st, continue in the row-ends on the longer side of the ear, sc in next 8 st, 3 sc in next st, continue in the row-ends on the shorter side of the ear, sc in next 5 st, inc in next st [28]
Fasten off and set aside.

Outer part (in orange yarn)
Ch 2. Crochet in rows.
Row 1 – 7: repeat the instructions for the inner part, but don't fasten off.
In the next row, we'll join the inner and outer parts together.
Row 8: ch 1, turn, place the inner part on top of your work with the wrong side facing up and crochet through both layers 6 7, sc in next 20 st, ch 1, turn [20] Leave the remaining stitches unworked.
Row 9: sc in all 20 st [20]
Fasten off, leaving an orange yarn tail for sewing. Weave in the other yarn ends 8.

LEFT EAR

Inner part (in amber yarn)
Ch 2. Crochet in rows.
Row 1: start in second ch from hook, inc in this ch, ch 1, turn [2]
Row 2: sc in next st, inc in next st, ch 1, turn [3]
Row 3: sc in next 2 st, inc in next st, ch 1, turn [4]
Row 4: sc in next 2 st, hdc in next st, dc inc in next st, ch 2, turn [5]
Row 5: dc inc in next st, dc in next st, hdc in next st, sc in next 2 st, ch 1, turn [6]
Row 6: sc in next 3 st, hdc inc in next st, dc in next st, dc inc in next st [8]
Next, we crochet around the ear.
Row 7: ch 1, turn, sc in next 7 st, 3 sc in next st, continue in the row-ends on the shorter side of the ear, sc in next 5 st, 3 sc in next st, continue in the row-ends on the longer side of the ear, sc in next 8 st, inc in next st [28]
Fasten off and set aside.

Outer part (in orange yarn)
Ch 2. Crochet in rows.
Row 1 – 7: repeat the instructions for the inner part, but don't fasten off.
In the next row, we'll join the inner and outer parts together.
Row 8: ch 1, turn, place the inner part on top of your work with the wrong side facing up and crochet through both layers, sc in next 20 st, ch 1, turn [20] Leave the remaining stitches unworked.
Row 9: sc in all 20 st [20]
Fasten off, leaving an orange yarn tail for sewing. Weave in all other yarn ends.

BODY (start in orange yarn)

Rnd 1: start 6 sc in a magic ring [6]
Rnd 2: inc in all 6 st [12]
Rnd 3: (sc in next st, inc in next st) repeat 6 times [18]
Rnd 4: (sc in next st, inc in next st, sc in next st) repeat 6 times [24]
Rnd 5: (sc in next 3 st, inc in next st) repeat 6 times [30]

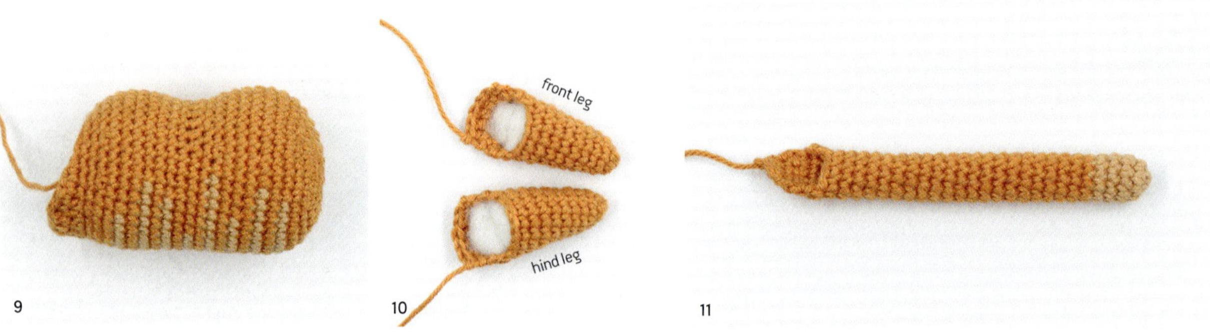

9 10 11

Rnd 6: (sc in next 2 st, inc in next st, sc in next 2 st) repeat 6 times [36]
Rnd 7: (sc in next 5 st, inc in next st) repeat 6 times [42]
In the next rounds, we'll alternate between orange and amber yarn. The color change is indicated in italics.
Rnd 8: sc in next 3 st, *(amber)* sc in next 15 st, *(orange)* sc in next 24 st [42]
Rnd 9: sc in all 42 st [42]
Rnd 10: sc in next 2 st, *(amber)* sc in next 17 st, *(orange)* sc in next 23 st [42]
Rnd 11: sc in all 42 st [42]
Sc in next st. This is the new start of the round.
Rnd 12: sc in next 4 st, *(amber)* sc in next 13 st, *(orange)* sc in next 25 st [42]
Rnd 13: sc in next 21 st, (sc in next 5 st, dec) repeat 3 times [39]
Rnd 14: sc in next st, *(amber)* sc in next 14 st, *(orange)* sc in next 6 st, (sc in next 2 st, dec, sc in next 2 st) repeat 3 times [36]
Rnd 15: sc in next 21 st, hdc in next 15 st [36]
Sc in next st. This is the new start of the round.
Rnd 16: sc in next 6 st, *(amber)* sc in next 14 st, *(orange)* sc in next 16 st [36]
Stuff the body with fiberfill and continue stuffing as you go.
Rnd 17: sc in next 21 st, (sc in next 2 st, inc in next st, sc in next 2 st) repeat 3 times [39]
Rnd 18: sc in next 3 st, *(amber)* sc in next 15 st, *(orange)* sc in next 21 st [39]
Rnd 19: sc in all 39 st [39]
Rnd 20: sc in next 2 st, *(amber)* sc in next 17 st, *(orange)* sc in next 20 st [39]
Rnd 21: sc in all 39 st [39]
Rnd 22: sc in next 5 st, *(amber)* sc in next 11 st, *(orange)* sc in next 23 st [39]
Continue crocheting in orange yarn.
Rnd 23: (sc in next 11 st, dec) repeat 3 times [36]
Rnd 24: (sc in next 2 st, dec, sc in next 2 st) repeat 6 times [30]
Rnd 25: (sc in next 4 st, dec, sc in next 4 st) repeat 3 times [27]
Rnd 26: sc in next 4 st, hdc in next 3 st, dc in next 3 st, hdc in next 3 st, sc in next 3 st [16] Leave the remaining stitches unworked.
Rnd 27: ch 1, turn, skip first sc, sc in next 3 st, hdc in next 2 st, dc in next 4 st, hdc in next 2 st, sc in next 3 st [14] Leave the remaining stitch unworked.
Fasten off, leaving a yarn tail for sewing 9.

FRONT LEG (make 2, in orange yarn)
Rnd 1: start 6 sc in a magic ring [6]
Rnd 2: (sc in next st, inc in next st) repeat 3 times [9]
Rnd 3: sc in next 4 st, inc in next st, sc in next 4 st [10]
Rnd 4: sc in next 9 st, inc in next st [11]
Rnd 5: sc in next 5 st, inc in next st, sc in next 5 st [12]
Rnd 6: sc in all 12 st [12]
Rnd 7: sc in next 11 st, inc in next st [13]
Rnd 8: sc in all 13 st [13]
Rnd 9: sc in next 6 st, inc in next st, sc in next 6 st [14]
Rnd 10: sc in all 14 st, ch 1, turn [14]
Continue crocheting in rows.

Row 11: skip first sc, sc in next 8 st, ch 1, turn [8] Leave the remaining stitches unworked.
Row 12: skip first sc, sc in next 7 st, ch 1, turn [7]
Row 13: skip first sc, sc in next st, hdc in next st, dc in next 2 st, hdc in next st, sc in next st [6]
Fasten off, leaving a yarn tail for sewing. Stuff the leg with fiberfill (10).

HIND LEG (make 2, in orange yarn)
Rnd 1: start 6 sc in a magic ring [6]
Rnd 2: (sc in next st, inc in next st) repeat 3 times [9]
Rnd 3: sc in next 4 st, inc in next st, sc in next 4 st [10]
Rnd 4: sc in next 9 st, inc in next st [11]
Rnd 5: sc in next 5 st, inc in next st, sc in next 5 st [12]
Rnd 6: sc in next 11 st, inc in next st [13]
Rnd 7: sc in next 6 st, inc in next st, sc in next 6 st [14]
Rnd 8: sc in next 13 st, inc in next st [15]
Rnd 9: sc in next 7 st, inc in next st, sc in next 7 st [16]
Rnd 10: sc in all 16 st, ch 1, turn [16]
Continue crocheting in rows.
Row 11: skip first sc, sc in next 9 st, ch 1, turn [9] Leave the remaining stitches unworked.
Row 12: skip first sc, sc in next 8 st, ch 1, turn [8]
Row 13: skip first sc, sc in next st, hdc in next st, dc in next 3 st, hdc in next st, sc in next st [7]
Fasten off, leaving a yarn tail for sewing. Stuff the leg with fiberfill (10).

TAIL (start in amber yarn)
Rnd 1: start 5 sc in a magic ring [5]
Rnd 2: inc in all 5 st [10]
Rnd 3 – 5: sc in all 10 st [10]
Change to orange yarn.
Rnd 6 – 26: sc in all 10 st [10]
Rnd 27: sc in all 10 st, ch 1, turn [10]
Continue crocheting in rows.
Row 28: skip first sc, sc in next 6 st, ch 1, turn [6] Leave the remaining stitches unworked.
Row 29: skip first sc, sc in next 5 st, ch 1, turn [5]
Row 30: skip first sc, sc in next 4 st, ch 1, turn [4]
Row 31: skip first sc, sc in next 3 st [3]
Fasten off, leaving a yarn tail for sewing (11).

12 13 14 15 16 17 18 19 20 21

ASSEMBLY

Make the eyes colorful

- Using several strands of green embroidery thread, embroider a line along the outer edge of each eye.
- Using black thread, embroider the upper outline and eyelashes (12).

Attach the snout

- Position the snout just below the eyes, with the stitch marker centered between them (13). Pin it in place, remove the stitch marker and sew around using the remaining yarn tail. Stuff the snout with fiberfill before closing the seam.
- Using black thread, embroider a nose between rounds 2-3 on the top side of the snout. Then add a short vertical line below the nose to create a T-shape (14).
- Cut the whiskers to the desired length. You get the cutest

look when each whisker is a slightly different length 14.

Attach the ears

- Position the ears on both sides of the head, between rounds 3-15 15 16. Pin them in place and sew them on using the remaining yarn tails 17.

Attach the head

- Lay the head on a flat surface, turned to the side so that one of the cat's ears is resting against the surface.
- Place the body next to the head. The longer side of the body (the side with the amber stripes) is the cat's back side. Pin the body to the head in this position 18.
- Check to see if the cat can lie down properly on its back. Adjust the position if needed and sew around using the remaining yarn tail.

Make a yarn ball

- Take a small amount of stuffing and some yarn.
- Wrap the yarn around the stuffing until the stuffing isn't visible anymore and the yarn ball is around 1.2" / 3 cm in diameter. Leave a yarn tail.

Attach the legs

- Place the front legs on the sides of the body, next to the neck seam. The front legs should point upward. Pin them in place.
- Place the hind legs on the sides of the body, on rounds 7-13. The hind legs should also point upward. Pin them in place 19 20.
- There should be some space left between the paws to insert the yarn ball. Check to see if the yarn ball fits in between, and adjust the position of the legs if needed.
- Sew around each leg using the remaining yarn tails.

Attach the tail

- Place the piece of wire or the pipe cleaner inside the tail.
- Place the tail at the back side of the body, pointing upward. Pin it in place and sew around using the remaining yarn tail 21.

ROSIE
the Siamese Cat

Skill level: ● ● ○
Size: 7" / 18 cm tall when made with the indicated yarn.

Amigurumi gallery: Scan or visit www.amigurumi.com/5513 to share pictures and find inspiration.

MATERIALS

• Sport weight yarn in cream, brown and dark brown • B-1 / 2.25 mm crochet hook • Safety eyes (11 mm) • White sewing thread *(for the whiskers)* • Black and light blue embroidery thread • Yarn needle • Pins • Stitch markers • Fiberfill for stuffing • Optional: Approx. 5.2" / 13 cm of wire or pipe cleaner *(for the tail if you want it to be posable)* • Optional: super fine weight mohair yarn in cream, brown and dark brown *(if you decide to crochet using two strands of yarn)*

NOTE

To achieve the soft texture shown in the photos, I crocheted with two strands held together: one strand of sport weight cotton and one strand of super fine weight mohair in a matching color. This is completely optional, using a single strand of yarn works just as well.

HEAD (start in dark brown yarn)
Rnd 1: start 6 sc in a magic ring [6]
Rnd 2: inc in all 6 st [12]
Rnd 3: (sc in next st, inc in next st) repeat 6 times [18]
Rnd 4: (sc in next st, inc in next st, sc in next st) repeat 6 times [24]
Rnd 5: (sc in next 3 st, inc in next st) repeat 6 times [30]
Rnd 6: (sc in next 2 st, inc in next st, sc in next 2 st) repeat 6 times [36]
Change to brown yarn.
Rnd 7: (sc in next 5 st, inc in next st) repeat 6 times [42]
Change to cream yarn.
Rnd 8: (sc in next 3 st, inc in next st, sc in next 3 st) repeat 6 times [48]
Insert the safety eyes between rounds 4 and 5, aligned with the magic ring. Note that the beginning of the round / the color changes should be at the bottom of the cat's face ❶.
Rnd 9 – 16: sc in all 48 st [48]
Rnd 17: (sc in next 3 st, dec, sc in next 3 st) repeat 6 times [42]
Rnd 18: (sc in next 5 st, dec) repeat 6 times [36]
Stuff the head with fiberfill and continue stuffing as you go.
Rnd 19: (sc in next 2 st, dec, sc in next 2 st) repeat 6 times [30]
Rnd 20: (sc in next 3 st, dec) repeat 6 times [24]
Rnd 21: (sc in next st, dec, sc in next st) repeat 6 times [18]
Rnd 22: (sc in next st, dec) repeat 6 times [12]
Rnd 23: dec 6 times [6]
Fasten off, leaving a yarn tail. Using a yarn needle, weave the yarn tail through the front loop of each remaining stitch and pull it tight to close. Weave in the yarn end.

SNOUT (in dark brown yarn)

Rnd 1: start 7 sc in a magic ring [7]
Rnd 2: inc in all 7 st [14]
Rnd 3: sc in next 10 st, hdc inc in next st, dc in next 3 st [15]
Rnd 4: dc in next 2 st, hdc inc in next st, sc in next 4 st *(mark the last sc with a stitch marker)*, sc in next 5 st [13] Leave the remaining stitches unworked.
Fasten off, leaving a yarn tail for sewing.

Attach the whiskers

Prepare 4 strands of white sewing thread, each about 6" / 15 cm long. Note that the stitch marker on the last round indicates the top center of the snout. With the wrong side of the snout facing you, tie 2 strands on the left and 2 strands on the right, keeping the knots on the inside so they remain hidden from the front 2. Each knot creates 2 loose ends, giving you 4 strands on each side. Pull each strand through a separate stitch gap to the front side of the snout 3.

RIGHT EAR

Inner part (in brown yarn)

Ch 2. Crochet in rows.
Row 1: start in second ch from hook, inc in this ch, ch 1, turn [2]
Row 2: sc in next st, inc in next st, ch 1, turn [3]
Row 3: sc in next 2 st, inc in next st, ch 2, turn [4]
Row 4: dc inc in next st, hdc in next st, sc in next 2 st, ch 1, turn [5]
Row 5: sc in next 2 st, hdc in next st, dc in next st, dc inc in next st, ch 2, turn [6]
Row 6: dc inc in next st, dc in next st, hdc inc in next st, sc in next 3 st [8]
Next, we crochet around the ear 4.
Row 7: ch 1, turn, sc in next 7 st, 3 sc in next st, continue in the row-ends on the longer side of the ear, sc in next 8 st, 3 sc in next st, continue in the row-ends on the shorter side of the ear, sc in next 5 st, inc in next st [28]
Fasten off and set aside 5.

Outer part (in dark brown yarn)
Ch 2. Crochet in rows.
Row 1 – 7: repeat the instructions for the inner part, but don't fasten off.
In the next row, we'll join the inner and outer parts together.
Row 8: ch 1, turn, place the inner part on top of your work with the wrong side facing up and crochet through both layers 6 7, sc in next 20 st, ch 1, turn [20] Leave the remaining stitches unworked.
Row 9: sc in all 20 st [20]
Fasten off, leaving a dark brown yarn tail for sewing. Weave in all other yarn ends.

LEFT EAR

Inner part (in brown yarn)
Ch 2. Crochet in rows.
Row 1: start in second ch from hook, inc in this ch, ch 1, turn [2]
Row 2: sc in next st, inc in next st, ch 1, turn [3]
Row 3: sc in next 2 st, inc in next st, ch 1, turn [4]
Row 4: sc in next 2 st, hdc in next st, dc inc in next st, ch 2, turn [5]
Row 5: dc inc in next st, dc in next st, hdc in next st, sc in next 2 st, ch 1, turn [6]
Row 6: sc in next 3 st, hdc inc in next st, dc in next st, dc inc in next st [8]
Next, we crochet around the ear.
Row 7: ch 1, turn, sc in next 7 st, 3 sc in next st, continue in the row-ends on the shorter side of the ear, sc in next 5 st, 3 sc in next st, continue in the row-ends on the longer side of the ear, sc in next 8 st, inc in next st [28]
Fasten off and set aside.

Outer part (in dark brown yarn)
Ch 2. Crochet in rows.
Row 1 – 7: repeat the instructions for the inner part, but don't fasten off.
In the next row, we'll join the inner and outer parts together.
Row 8: ch 1, turn, place the inner part on top of your work with the wrong side facing up and crochet through both layers, sc in next 20 st, ch 1, turn [20] Leave the remaining stitches unworked.
Row 9: sc in all 20 st [20]
Fasten off, leaving a dark brown yarn tail for sewing. Weave in all other yarn ends 8.

BODY (in cream yarn)

Lower part
Rnd 1: start 7 sc in a magic ring [7]
Rnd 2: inc in all 7 st [14]
Rnd 3: (sc in next st, inc in next st) repeat 7 times [21]
Rnd 4: (sc in next st, inc in next st, sc in next st) repeat 7 times [28]
Rnd 5: (sc in next 3 st, inc in next st) repeat 7 times [35]
Rnd 6: (sc in next 2 st, inc in next st, sc in next 2 st) repeat 7 times [42]
Rnd 7: (sc in next 5 st, inc in next st) repeat 7 times [49]
Rnd 8: (sc in next 3 st, inc in next st, sc in next 3 st) repeat 7 times [56]
Rnd 9: (sc in next 7 st, inc in next st) repeat 7 times [63]
Rnd 10 – 22: sc in all 63 st [63]
Rnd 23: sc in next 61 st, dec [62]
Rnd 24: sc in next 30 st, dec, sc in next 30 st [61]
Rnd 25: sc in next 45 st, dec, sc in next 14 st [60]
Rnd 26: sc in next 14 st, dec, sc in next 44 st [59]
Rnd 27: sc in next 57 st, dec [58]
Stuff the lower part with fiberfill and continue stuffing as you go.
Rnd 28: sc in next 28 st, dec, sc in next 28 st [57]
Rnd 29: sc in next 13 st, dec, sc in next 42 st [56]
Rnd 30: sc in next 41 st, dec, sc in next 13 st [55]
Rnd 31: sc in next 53 st, dec [54]
Rnd 32: sc in next 26 st, dec, sc in next 26 st [53]
Rnd 33: sc in next 11 st, dec, sc in next 40 st [52]
Rnd 34: sc in next 39 st, dec, sc in next 11 st [51]
Rnd 35: sc in next 49 st, dec [50]
Rnd 36: (sc in next 23 st, dec) repeat 2 times [48]
Rnd 37: (sc in next 3 st, dec, sc in next 3 st) repeat 6 times [42]

Rnd 38: (sc in next 5 st, dec) repeat 6 times [36]
Rnd 39: (sc in next 2 st, dec, sc in next 2 st) repeat 6 times [30]
Rnd 40: (sc in next 3 st, dec) repeat 6 times [24]
Rnd 41: (sc in next st, dec, sc in next st) repeat 6 times [18]
Rnd 42: (sc in next st, dec) repeat 6 times [12]
Rnd 43: dec 6 times [6]
Fasten off, leaving a yarn tail. Using a yarn needle, weave the yarn tail through the front loop of each remaining stitch and pull it tight to close. Weave in the yarn end.

Upper part

Rnd 1: start 6 sc in a magic ring [6]
Rnd 2: inc in all 6 st [12]
Rnd 3: (sc in next st, inc in next st) repeat 6 times [18]
Rnd 4: (sc in next st, inc in next st, sc in next st) repeat 6 times [24]
Rnd 5: (sc in next 3 st, inc in next st) repeat 6 times [30]
Rnd 6: (sc in next 2 st, inc in next st, sc in next 2 st) repeat

12

6 times [36]
Rnd 7: (sc in next 5 st, inc in next st) repeat 6 times [42]
Rnd 8: (sc in next 3 st, inc in next st, sc in next 3 st) repeat 6 times [48]
Rnd 9 – 12: sc in all 48 st [48]
Rnd 13: sc in next 13 st, hdc in next 2 st, hdc inc in next st, dc in next 16 st, hdc inc in next st, hdc in next 2 st, sc in next 13 st [50]
Rnd 14: sc in next 15 st, hdc in next 2 st, dc inc in next st, dc in next 14 st, dc inc in next st, hdc in next 2 st, sc in next 15 st [52]
Rnd 15: sc in next 26 st *(mark the last sc with a stitch marker)*, sc in next 26 st [52]
Fasten off, leaving a yarn tail for sewing. Stuff the upper part lightly with fiberfill 9.

NECK (in cream yarn)

Ch 27.
Rnd 1: start in first ch to form a circle *(make sure the chains aren't twisted)*, sc in all 27 ch [27] 10
Rnd 2: (sc in next 7 st, dec) repeat 3 times [24]
Rnd 3: (sc in next 3 st, inc in next st) repeat 6 times [30]
Rnd 4: (sc in next 2 st, inc in next st, sc in next 2 st) repeat 6 times [36]
Sc in next 2 st. Fasten off, leaving a yarn tail for sewing 11.

FRONT LEG (make 2, start in dark brown yarn)

Rnd 1: start 6 sc in a magic ring [6]
Rnd 2: inc in all 6 st [12]
Rnd 3 – 8: sc in all 12 st [12]
Rnd 9: sc in next 11 st, inc in next st [13]
Rnd 10: sc in all 13 st [13]

Rnd 11: sc in next 6 st, inc in next st, sc in next 6 st [14]
Stuff the leg with fiberfill and continue stuffing as you go.
Rnd 12 – 13: sc in all 14 st [14]
Change to brown yarn.
Rnd 14 – 15: sc in all 14 st [14]
Change to cream yarn.
Rnd 16 – 20: sc in all 14 st [14]
Rnd 21: sc in next 13 st, ch 1, turn [13] Leave the remaining stitch unworked.
Continue crocheting in rows.
Row 22: skip first sc, sc in next 10 st, ch 1, turn [10] Leave the remaining stitches unworked.
Row 23: skip first sc, sc in next 9 st, ch 1, turn [9]
Row 24: skip first sc, sc in next 8 st, ch 1, turn [8]
Row 25: skip first sc, sc in next 7 st, ch 1, turn [7]
Row 26: skip first sc, sc in next 6 st, ch 1, turn [6]
Row 27: skip first sc, sc in next 5 st, ch 1, turn [5]
Row 28: skip first sc, sc in next 4 st [4]
Fasten off, leaving a yarn tail for sewing (12).

HIND LEG (make 2)

Foot (in dark brown yarn)

Rnd 1: start 6 sc in a magic ring [6]
Rnd 2: inc in all 6 st [12]
Rnd 3 – 6: sc in all 12 st [12]
Rnd 7: sc in all 12 st, ch 1, turn [12]
Continue crocheting in rows.
Row 8: skip first sc, sc in next 7 st, ch 1, turn [7] Leave the remaining stitches unworked.
Row 9: skip first sc, sc in next 6 st, ch 1, turn [6]
Row 10: skip first sc, sc in next 5 st, ch 1, turn [5]
Row 11: skip first sc, sc in next 4 st [4]
Fasten off, leaving a yarn tail for sewing. Stuff the feet with fiberfill (13).

Upper part (in cream yarn)

Rnd 1: start 6 sc in a magic ring [6]
Rnd 2: inc in all 6 st [12]
Rnd 3: (sc in next st, inc in next st) repeat 6 times [18]
Rnd 4: (sc in next st, inc in next st, sc in next st) repeat 6 times [24]
Rnd 5: (sc in next 3 st, inc in next st) repeat 6 times [30]
Rnd 6: (sc in next 2 st, inc in next st, sc in next 2 st) repeat 6 times [36]
Rnd 7: (sc in next 5 st, inc in next st) repeat 6 times [42]
Rnd 8: (sc in next 3 st, inc in next st, sc in next 3 st) repeat 6 times [48]
Rnd 9: (sc in next 7 st, inc in next st) repeat 6 times [54]
Fasten off, leaving a yarn tail for sewing.

TAIL (start in dark brown yarn)

Rnd 1: start 5 sc in a magic ring [5]
Rnd 2: inc in all 5 st [10]
Rnd 3 – 30: sc in all 10 st [10]
Change to brown yarn.
Rnd 31 – 37: sc in all 10 st [10]
Sc in next st. This is the new start of the round.
Change to cream yarn.
Rnd 38: sc in all 10 st [10]
Rnd 39: sc in next 9 st, ch 1, turn [9] Leave the remaining stitch unworked.
Continue crocheting in rows.
Row 40: skip first sc, sc in next 6 st, ch 1, turn [6] Leave the remaining stitches unworked.
Row 41: skip first sc, sc in next 5 st, ch 1, turn [5]
Row 42: skip first sc, sc in next 4 st, ch 1, turn [4]
Row 43: skip first sc, sc in next 3 st [3]
Fasten off, leaving a yarn tail for sewing (14).

ASSEMBLY

Make the eyes colorful

- Using several strands of light blue thread, embroider a line along the outer edge of each eye (15).
- Using black thread, embroider the upper outline and the eyelashes (15).

Attach the snout

- Position the snout just below the eyes, with the stitch marker

centered between them (16). Pin the snout in place, remove the stitch marker and sew around using the remaining yarn tail. Stuff the snout with fiberfill before closing the seam.

- Using black thread, embroider a nose covering round 2 of the top side of the snout.
- Cut the whiskers to the desired length. You get the cutest look when each whisker is a slightly different length (17).

Attach the ears

- Position the ears on both sides of the head, between rounds 13-16 (18) (19). Pin them in place and sew them on using the remaining yarn tails (20).

Assemble the body

- Place the upper part of the body on top of the lower part (21).
- The stitch marker on the upper part indicates the center of the back and should be aligned with round 38 of the lower part.

- The front side of the upper part should be positioned on round 29 of the lower part of the body.
- Pin it in place and sew around using the remaining yarn tail.

Attach the front legs

- Place the front legs on the body with the longer sides of the leg (crocheted in rows) facing outward and the paws facing downward. The opening of the legs should cover the seam where the upper and lower parts of the body were joined.
- Pin the front legs in place and check to see if the cat can sit properly. Adjust the position if needed and sew around using the remaining yarn tails 22.

Attach the hind legs

- Pin the upper parts of the hind legs on the lower sides of the body. Do this while your cat is sitting on a flat surface. The upper parts of the legs should cover rounds 7-24 of the lower part of the body. Sew around using the remaining yarn tails. Stuff with fiberfill before closing the seam 23.
- Place the feet below the upper parts of the hind legs. The feet should be facing the front side of the cat. Pin them in place and sew around using the remaining yarn tails 24.

Attach the neck

- Pin the neck on top of the body with round 4 at the bottom. Sew around using the remaining yarn tail 25.
- Stuff the neck with fiberfill.

Attach the head

- Place the head on top of the neck. Turn the head slightly to the side to give your cat a cuter look. Pin it in place and sew around using the remaining yarn tail.

Attach the tail

- If you want the tail to be posable, insert the wire or pipe cleaner. Otherwise, lightly stuff it with fiberfill.
- Position the tail to the back of the body, with the tail pointing to the same side your cat is looking at. Pin it in place and sew around using the remaining yarn tail.
- Slightly bend the tail upward to give your cat a cuter look.

BONNIE
the Saint Bernard

Skill level: ● ● ○
Size: 5" / 12.5 cm tall when made with the indicated yarn.

Amigurumi gallery: Scan or visit www.amigurumi.com/5514 to share pictures and find inspiration.

MATERIALS

• Sport weight yarn in orange, brown, dark brown and white • B-1 / 2.25 mm crochet hook • Safety eyes (8 mm) • Black and white embroidery thread • Yarn needle • Pins • Stitch markers • Fiberfill for stuffing • Optional: White sewing thread *(for the assembly tip)*

HEAD (start in orange yarn)

Rnd 1: start 6 sc in a magic ring [6]
Rnd 2: inc in all 6 st [12]
Rnd 3: (sc in next st, inc in next st) repeat 6 times [18]
Rnd 4: (sc in next st, inc in next st, sc in next st) repeat 6 times [24]
Rnd 5: (sc in next 3 st, inc in next st) repeat 6 times [30]
Rnd 6: (sc in next 2 st, inc in next st, sc in next 2 st) repeat 6 times [36]
Rnd 7: (sc in next 5 st, inc in next st) repeat 6 times [42]
Rnd 8: (sc in next 3 st, inc in next st, sc in next 3 st) repeat 6 times [48]
Rnd 9: sc in all 48 st [48]

In the next rounds, we'll alternate between orange and brown yarn. The color change is indicated in italics.

Rnd 10: sc in next 18 st, *(brown)* sc in next 4 st, *(orange)* sc in next 4 st, *(brown)* sc in next 4 st, *(orange)* sc in next 18 st [48]
Rnd 11: sc in next 17 st, *(brown)* sc in next 6 st, *(orange)* sc in next 2 st, *(brown)* sc in next 6 st, *(orange)* sc in next 17 st [48]
Rnd 12 – 14: sc in next 16 st, *(brown)* sc in next 16 st, *(orange)* sc in next 16 st [48]
Rnd 15: sc in next 17 st, *(brown)* sc in next 15 st, *(orange)* sc in next 16 st [48]
Rnd 16: sc in next 18 st, *(brown)* sc in next 13 st, *(orange)* sc in next 17 st [48]
Rnd 17: sc in next 19 st, *(brown)* sc in next 12 st, *(orange)* sc in next 17 st [48]

In the next rounds, we'll alternate between orange and white yarn. The color change is indicated in italics.

Rnd 18: sc in next 22 st, *(white)* sc in next 7 st, *(orange)* sc in next 19 st [48]

The center of the white patch is the center of the puppy's face. Insert the safety eyes between rounds 12 and 13, with an interspace of 7 stitches ❶.

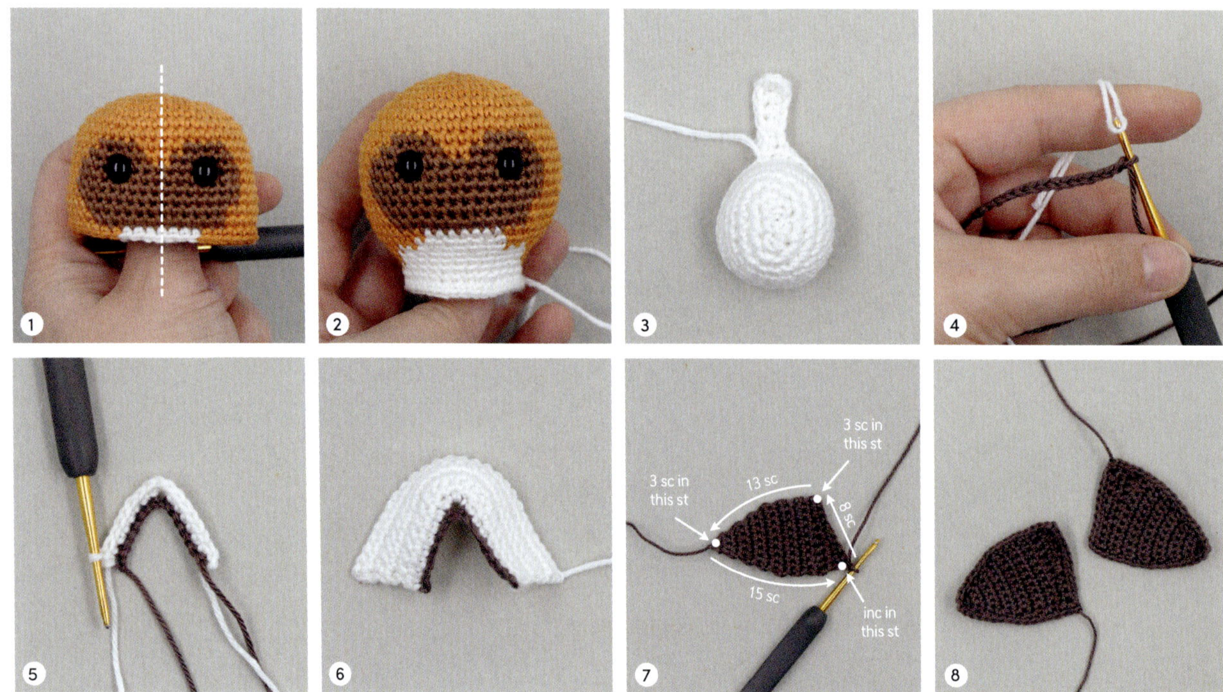

Stuff the head with fiberfill and continue stuffing as you go.

Rnd 19: (sc in next 3 st, dec, sc in next 3 st) repeat 2 times, sc in next 3 st, dec, *(white)* sc in next 6 st, dec, sc in next st, *(orange)* sc in next 2 st, (sc in next 3 st, dec, sc in next 3 st) repeat 2 times [42]

Rnd 20: (sc in next 5 st, dec) repeat 2 times, sc in next 2 st, *(white)* sc in next 3 st, dec, sc in next 5 st, dec, sc in next st, *(orange)* sc in next 4 st, dec, sc in next 5 st, dec [36]

Rnd 21: (sc in next 2 st, dec, sc in next 2 st) repeat 2 times, sc in next st, *(white)* sc in next st, (dec, sc in next 4 st) repeat 2 times, *(orange)* dec, sc in next 4 st, dec, sc in next 2 st [30]

Rnd 22: sc in next 11 st, *(white)* sc in next 11 st, *(orange)* sc in next 8 st [30]

Rnd 23: sc in next 10 st, *(white)* sc in next 13 st, *(orange)* sc in next 7 st [30]

Rnd 24: sc in next 9 st, *(white)* inc in next st, (sc in next 9 st, inc in next st) repeat 2 times [33]

Continue crocheting in white yarn.

Rnd 25: (sc in next 5 st, inc in next st, sc in next 5 st) repeat 3 times [36]

Fasten off, leaving a yarn tail for sewing (2).

EYELID (make 2, in brown yarn)

Ch 5. Crochet in rows.

Row 1: start in second ch from hook, slst in this ch, sc in next 2 ch, slst in last ch [4]

Fasten off, leaving a yarn tail for sewing.

SNOUT (in white yarn)

Leave a starting yarn tail. Ch 4. Stitches are worked around both sides of the foundation chain.

Rnd 1: start in second ch from hook, inc in this ch, sc in next ch, 4 sc in last ch. Continue on the other side of the foundation chain, sc in next ch, inc in last ch [10]

Rnd 2: inc in next 2 st, sc in next st, inc in next 4 st, sc in next st, inc in next 2 st [18]

Rnd 3: sc in next st, inc in next st, sc in next 5 st, inc in next st, sc in next 2 st, inc in next st, sc in next 5 st, inc in next st, sc in next st [22]

Using a yarn needle, weave the starting yarn tail through the foundation chain to hide the stitch gaps.

Rnd 4 – 5: sc in all 22 st [22]

Rnd 6: sc in next 9 st, hdc inc in next st, hdc in next 3 st, hdc inc in next st, sc in next 8 st [24]

Rnd 7: sc in next 8 st, hdc in next 5 st, hdc inc in next st, hdc in next 4 st, sc in next 6 st [25]

In the next round, we'll make the stripe that covers the puppy's forehead.

Rnd 8: sc in next 2 st, ch 8, start in third ch from hook, dc in next 2 ch, hdc in next 2 ch, sc in next 2 ch, continue on the snout, slst in next st [9] Leave the remaining stitches unworked.

Fasten off, leaving a yarn tail for sewing. Stuff the snout with fiberfill 3.

SNOUT COVER (start in dark brown yarn)

Ch 15. Fasten off.

Pull up a loop of white yarn in the first chain. Crochet in rows 4. Work the first stitch in the same chain where you attached the yarn.

Row 1: ch 1, sc in next 7 ch, 3 sc in next ch, sc in next 7 ch, ch 1, turn [17] 5

Row 2: sc in next 7 st, inc in next 3 st, sc in next 7 st, ch 1, turn [20]

Row 3: sc in next 7 st, (sc in next st, inc in next st) repeat 3 times, sc in next 7 st, ch 1, turn [23]

Row 4: inc in next st, sc in next 21 st, inc in next st, ch 1, turn [25]

Row 5: sc in all 25 st, ch 1, turn [25]

Row 6: inc in next st, sc in next 23 st, inc in next st [27]

Fasten off, leaving a white yarn tail for sewing. Weave in all other yarn ends 6.

RIGHT EAR (in dark brown yarn)

Ch 2. Crochet in rows.

Row 1: start in second ch from hook, inc in this ch, ch 1, turn [2]

Row 2: sc in next st, inc in next st, ch 1, turn [3]

Row 3: sc in next 2 st, inc in next st, ch 1, turn [4]

Row 4: sc in next 3 st, inc in next st, ch 1, turn [5]

Row 5: sc in next 4 st, inc in next st, ch 1, turn [6]

Row 6: sc in next 5 st, inc in next st, ch 1, turn [7]

Row 7: sc in next 6 st, inc in next st, ch 1, turn [8]

Row 8: sc in next 7 st, inc in next st, ch 1, turn [9]

Row 9 – 11: sc in all 9 st, ch 1, turn [9]

Row 12: sc in all 9 st, ch 2, turn [9]

Row 13: dc in next 3 st, hdc in next 3 st, sc in next 3 st, ch 1, turn [9]

Row 14: sc in next 4 st, hdc in next 2 st, dc in next 3 st [9]

Next, we crochet around the ear 7.

Row 15: ch 1, turn, sc in next 8 st, 3 sc in next st, continue in the row-ends on the shorter side of the ear, sc in next 13 st, 3 sc in next st, continue in the row-ends on the longer side of the ear, sc in next 15 st, inc in next st [44]

Fasten off, leaving a yarn tail for sewing.

LEFT EAR (in dark brown yarn)

Ch 2. Crochet in rows.

Row 1 – 11: repeat the instructions for the right ear.

Row 12: sc in all 9 st, ch 1, turn [9]

Row 13: sc in next 3 st, hdc in next 3 st, dc in next 3 st, ch 2, turn [9]

Row 14: dc in next 3 st, hdc in next 2 st, sc in next 4 st [9]

Next, we crochet around the ear.

Row 15: ch 1, turn, sc in next 8 st, 3 sc in next st, continue in the row-ends on the longer side of the ear, sc in next 15 st, 3 sc in next st, continue in the row-ends on the shorter side of the ear, sc in next 13 st, inc in next st [44]

Fasten off, leaving a yarn tail for sewing 8.

BODY (start in white yarn)

Rnd 1: start 6 sc in a magic ring [6]

Rnd 2: inc in all 6 st [12]

Rnd 3: (sc in next st, inc in next st) repeat 6 times [18]

Rnd 4: (sc in next st, inc in next st, sc in next st) repeat 6 times [24]

9

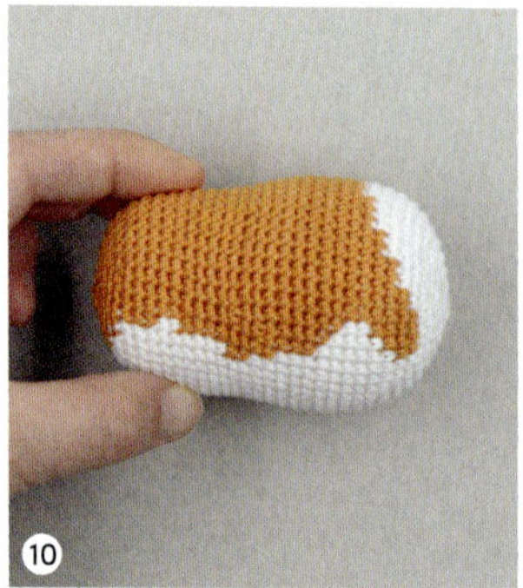
10

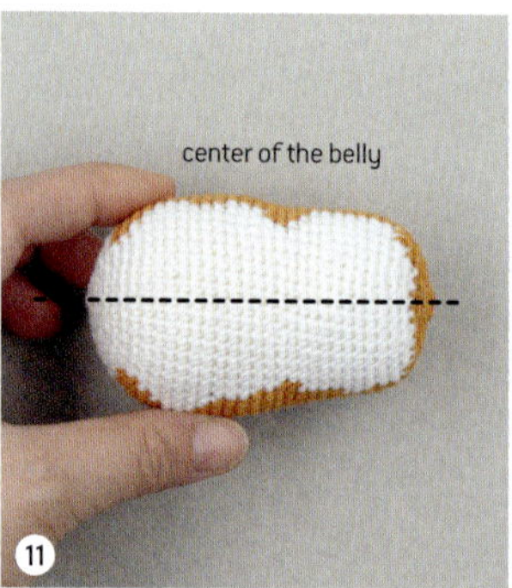

11

12

Rnd 5: (sc in next 3 st, inc in next st) repeat 6 times [30]
Rnd 6: (sc in next 2 st, inc in next st, sc in next 2 st) repeat 6 times [36]

In the next rounds, we'll alternate between white and orange yarn. The color change is indicated in italics.

Rnd 7: sc in next 4 st, inc in next st, *(orange)* sc in next 4 st, *(white)* sc in next 2 st, inc in next st, (sc in next 5 st, inc in next st) repeat 2 times, sc in next 4 st, *(orange)* sc in next st, inc in next st, sc in next st, *(white)* sc in next 4 st, inc in next st [42]
Rnd 8: sc in next 3 st, inc in next st, sc in next 2 st, *(orange)* sc in next 4 st, inc in next st, *(white)* sc in next 3 st, (sc in next 3 st, inc in next st, sc in next 3 st) repeat 2 times, sc in next 3 st, *(orange)* inc in next st, sc in next 4 st, *(white)* sc in next 2 st, inc in next st, sc in next 3 st [48]
Rnd 9: sc in next 8 st, *(orange)* sc in next 7 st, *(white)* sc in next 18 st, *(orange)* sc in next 7 st, *(white)* sc in next 8 st [48]
Rnd 10: sc in next 9 st, *(orange)* sc in next 8 st, *(white)* sc in next 14 st, *(orange)* sc in next 8 st, *(white)* sc in next 9 st [48]
Rnd 11: sc in next 10 st, *(orange)* sc in next 10 st, *(white)* sc in next 8 st, *(orange)* sc in next 10 st, *(white)* sc in next 10 st [48]
Rnd 12: sc in next 10 st, *(orange)* sc in next 28 st, *(white)* sc in next 10 st [48] 9
Rnd 13: sc in next 10 st, *(orange)* sc in next 29 st, *(white)* sc in next 9 st [48]
Rnd 14: sc in next 9 st, *(orange)* sc in next 31 st, *(white)* sc in next 8 st [48]
Rnd 15 – 16: sc in next 9 st, *(orange)* sc in next 32 st, *(white)* sc in next 7 st [48]
Rnd 17: sc in next 10 st, *(orange)* sc in next 31 st, *(white)* sc in next 7 st [48]
Rnd 18: sc in next 10 st, *(orange)* sc in next 32 st, *(white)* sc in next 6 st [48]
Rnd 19: sc in next 7 st, dec, sc in next st, *(orange)* sc in next 13 st, dec, sc in next 14 st, dec, sc in next st, *(white)* sc in next 6 st [45]
Rnd 20: sc in next 8 st, *(orange)* sc in next 5 st, dec, sc in next 13 st, dec, sc in next 10 st, *(white)* sc in next 3 st, dec [42]
Rnd 21: sc in next 6 st, dec, *(orange)* (sc in next 12 st, dec) repeat 2 times, sc in next 2 st, *(white)* sc in next 4 st [39]
Rnd 22: sc in next 8 st, *(orange)* sc in next 26 st, *(white)* sc in next 5 st [39]

Stuff the body with fiberfill and continue stuffing as you go.

Rnd 23: sc in next 9 st, *(orange)* sc in next 25 st, *(white)* sc in next 5 st [39]
Rnd 24: sc in next 10 st, *(orange)* sc in next 24 st, *(white)* sc in next 5 st [39]
Rnd 25: sc in next 6 st, inc in next st, sc in next 3 st, *(orange)* sc in next 9 st, inc in next st, sc in next 12 st, inc in next st, sc in next st, *(white)* sc in next 5 st [42]
Rnd 26 – 27: sc in next 11 st, *(orange)* sc in next 25 st, *(white)* sc in next 6 st [42]
Rnd 28 – 30: sc in next 11 st, *(orange)* sc in next 26 st, *(white)* sc in next 5 st [42]
Rnd 31: sc in next 5 st, dec, sc in next 2 st, *(orange)* sc in next 3 st, dec, (sc in next 5 st, dec) repeat 3 times, sc in next 4 st, *(white)* sc in next st, dec [36]
Rnd 32: sc in next 2 st, dec, sc in next 2 st, *(orange)* (sc in next

2 st, dec, sc in next 2 st) repeat 5 times [30]
Continue crocheting in orange yarn.
Rnd 33: sc in next 2 st, dec, sc in next st, (sc in next 3 st, dec) repeat 5 times [24]
Rnd 34: (sc in next st, dec, sc in next st) repeat 6 times [18]
Rnd 35: (sc in next st, dec) repeat 6 times [12]
Rnd 36: dec 6 times [6]
Fasten off, leaving a yarn tail. Using a yarn needle, weave the yarn tail through the front loop of each remaining stitch and pull it tight to close 10 11.

FRONT LEG (make 2, in white yarn)
Rnd 1: start 6 sc in a magic ring [6]
Rnd 2: inc in all 6 st [12]
Rnd 3: (sc in next 3 st, inc in next st) repeat 3 times [15]
Rnd 4 – 11: sc in all 15 st [15]
Rnd 12: sc in next 7 st, inc in next st, sc in next 7 st [16]
Rnd 13: sc in next 15 st, inc in next st, ch 1, turn [17]
Continue crocheting in rows.
Row 14: skip first sc, sc in next 11 st, ch 1, turn [11] Leave the remaining stitches unworked.
Row 15: skip first sc, sc in next 10 st, ch 1, turn [10]
Row 16: skip first sc, sc in next 9 st, ch 1, turn [9]
Row 17: skip first sc, sc in next 8 st, ch 1, turn [8]
Row 18: skip first sc, sc in next st, hdc in next st, dc in next 3 st, hdc in next st, sc in next st [7]
Fasten off, leaving a yarn tail for sewing. Stuff the front legs with fiberfill 12.

HIND LEG (make 2)

Upper part (in orange yarn)
Rnd 1: start 7 sc in a magic ring [7]
Rnd 2: inc in all 7 st [14]
Rnd 3: (sc in next st, inc in next st) repeat 7 times [21]
Rnd 4: (sc in next st, inc in next st, sc in next st) repeat 7 times [28]
Rnd 5: (sc in next 3 st, inc in next st) repeat 7 times [35]
Rnd 6: (sc in next 2 st, inc in next st, sc in next 2 st) repeat 7 times [42]

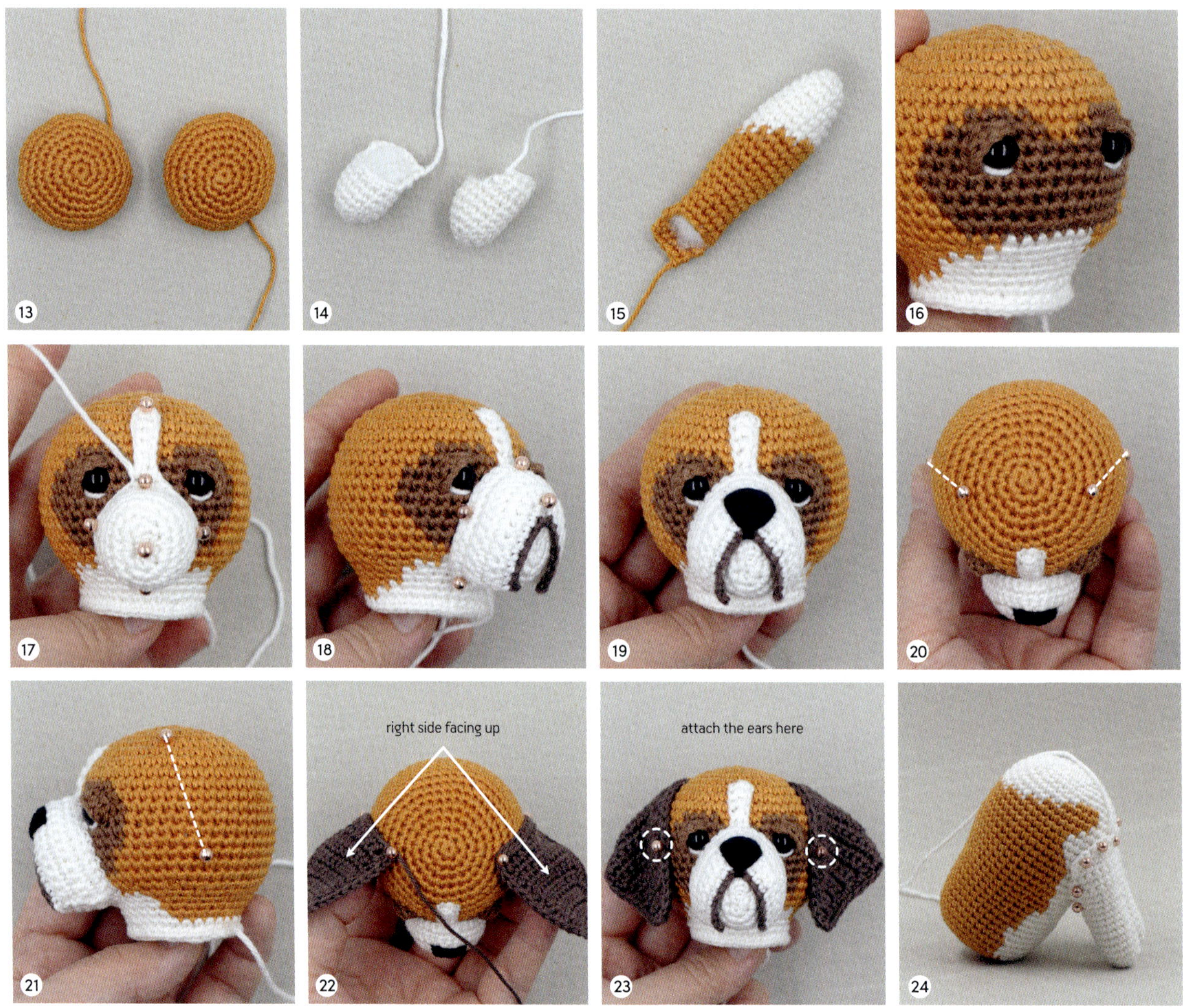

Rnd 7: (sc in next 5 st, inc in next st) repeat 7 times [49]
Rnd 8: sc in all 49 st [49]
Rnd 9: (sc in next 5 st, dec) repeat 7 times [42]
Rnd 10: (sc in next 2 st, dec, sc in next 2 st) repeat 7 times [35]
Rnd 11: (sc in next 3 st, dec) repeat 7 times [28]
Rnd 12: (sc in next st, dec, sc in next st) repeat 7 times [21]
Stuff lightly with fiberfill. The upper part of the leg should have some volume, but also remain quite flat.
Rnd 13: (sc in next st, dec) repeat 7 times [14]
Rnd 14: dec 7 times [7]
Fasten off, leaving a yarn tail. Using a yarn needle, weave the yarn tail through the front loop of each remaining stitch and pull it tight to close. Leave a yarn tail for sewing 13.

Foot (in white yarn)
Rnd 1: start 6 sc in a magic ring [6]
Rnd 2: inc in all 6 st [12]
Rnd 3: (sc in next 3 st, inc in next st) repeat 3 times [15]

Rnd 4 – 6: sc in all 15 st [15]
Rnd 7: sc in all 15 st, ch 1, turn [15]
Continue crocheting in rows.
Row 8: skip first sc, sc in next 8 st, ch 1, turn [8] Leave the remaining stitches unworked.
Row 9: skip first sc, sc in next st, hdc in next 2 st, dc in next st, hdc in next 2 st, sc in next st [7]
Fasten off, leaving a yarn tail for sewing. Stuff the feet with fiberfill (14).

TAIL (start in white yarn)
Rnd 1: start 6 sc in a magic ring [6]
Rnd 2: (inc in next 2 st, sc in next st) repeat 2 times [10]
Rnd 3: (sc in next 2 st, inc in next st, sc in next 2 st) repeat 2 times [12]
Rnd 4: (sc in next 5 st, inc in next st) repeat 2 times [14]
Rnd 5: (sc in next 3 st, inc in next st, sc in next 3 st) repeat 2 times [16]
Rnd 6: sc in next 15 st, inc in next st [17]
Rnd 7: sc in next 8 st, inc in next st, sc in next 8 st [18]
In the next rounds, we'll alternate between white and orange yarn. The color change is indicated in italics.
Rnd 8: sc in next 7 st, *(orange)* sc in next 4 st, *(white)* sc in next 7 st [18]
Rnd 9: sc in next 5 st, *(orange)* sc in next 8 st, *(white)* sc in next 5 st [18]
Rnd 10: sc in next 4 st, *(orange)* sc in next 10 st, *(white)* sc in next 4 st [18]
Rnd 11: sc in next 3 st, *(orange)* sc in next 15 st [18]
Continue crocheting in orange yarn.
Rnd 12 – 13: sc in all 18 st [18]
Stuff the tail with fiberfill and continue stuffing as you go.
Rnd 14: (sc in next 7 st, dec) repeat 2 times [16]
Rnd 15: sc in next 14 st, dec [15]
Rnd 16: sc in next 6 st, dec, sc in next 7 st [14]
Rnd 17: sc in next 12 st, dec [13]
Rnd 18: sc in next 5 st, dec, sc in next 6 st [12]
Rnd 19 – 20: sc in all 12 st [12]
Rnd 21: sc in next 6 st, ch 1, turn [6] Leave the remaining stitches unworked.
Continue crocheting in rows.
Row 22: skip first sc, sc in next 6 st, ch 1, turn [6] Leave the remaining stitches unworked.
Row 23: skip first sc, sc in next 5 st, ch 1, turn [5]
Row 24: skip first sc, sc in next 4 st [4]
Fasten off, leaving a yarn tail for sewing (15).

ASSEMBLY

TIP: *Sewing white pieces onto the orange and brown parts can be challenging. To make the seams less noticeable, try using white sewing thread and a thin needle instead of the yarn tails.*

Assemble the eyes

- Using several strands of white thread, embroider a line below the eyes (16).
- Sew the eyelids above the safety eyes (16).

Attach the snout

- Pin the snout in place just below the safety eyes, aligning the stripe with the center of the forehead. Sew it on using the remaining yarn tail (17).
- Place the snout cover on top of the snout with the dark brown line facing the front. Pin it in place, then sew around the white section using the remaining yarn tail. Leave the brown line unsewn (18).

Embroider the nose

- Using a strand of black thread, embroider the nose on rows 1-3 of the snout cover, aligned with the forehead stripe (19).

Attach the ears

- Position the ears on both sides of the head, between rounds 6-16 (20) (21), with the right side facing up (22). Pin them in place and sew them on using the remaining yarn tails.
- Bend the ears down and sew them to the face to secure the position (23).

25

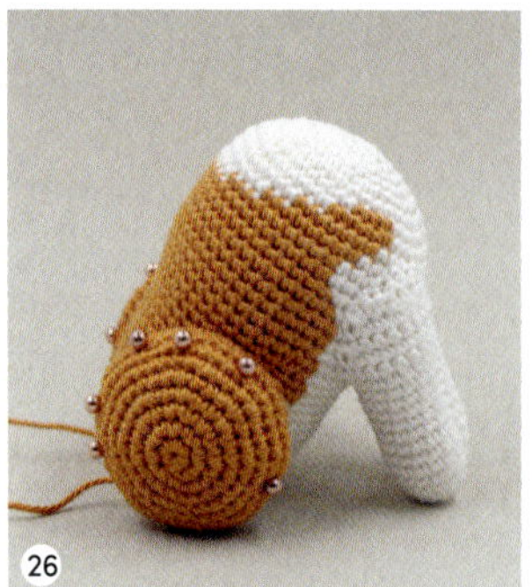

26

27

28

Attach the front legs

- Place the front legs on the front side of the body, on rounds 9-18. They should be aligned with the dog's belly (the white side of the body).
- Pin them in place and check to see if the puppy can sit properly. Adjust the position if needed and sew around using the remaining yarn tails 24 25.

Attach the hind legs

- Place the upper parts of the hind legs on the lower sides of the body. It's easiest to do this while your dog is sitting on a flat surface. The upper parts should cover rounds 20-32 of the body. Pin them in place and sew around using the remaining yarn tails 26 27.
- Place the feet below the upper parts of the hind legs. The feet should be facing the front side of the dog. Pin them in place and sew around using the remaining yarn tails 28 29.

Attach the tail

- Pin the tail on the back side of the body, pointing to the same side you want your dog to look at. Sew around using the remaining yarn tail 30.
- Bend the tail to the side and sew it to the upper part of the hind leg to secure the position.

Attach the head

- Pin the head on top of the body. Turn the head slightly to the side (the same direction as the tail) to give your dog a cuter look. Sew around using the remaining yarn tail.

29

30

31

32

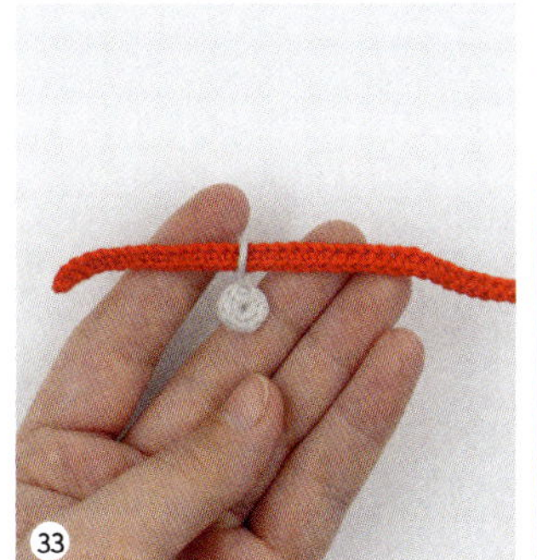
33

34

How to make a COLLAR for your favorite cat or dog

This collar suits all cats & dogs in this book!

MEDALLION (in gray yarn)

Rnd 1: start 8 sc in a magic ring [8]

Fasten off with an invisible join. Create a loop with the remaining yarn tail and knot it to secure. Weave in the remaining yarn tails (31).

BELT (in red yarn)

Wrap a strand of yarn around the neck of the cat or dog to measure its size. Make a chain about 2 cm longer than the circumference of the neck. Wrap it around the neck to ensure it fits comfortably (32).

Starting in the second chain from the hook, work 1 sc in each chain.

Fasten off and leave a yarn tail for sewing.

ASSEMBLY

- Run the belt through the loop of the medallion (33).
- Wrap the collar around the dog's or cat's neck and join the ends together using the remaining yarn tail (34). Weave in the remaining yarn ends.

MISTY
the Turkish Angora

Skill level: ● ● ●
Size: 4.5" / 11 cm tall when made with the indicated yarn.

Amigurumi gallery: Scan or visit www.amigurumi.com/5515 to share pictures and find inspiration.

MATERIALS

• Sport weight yarn in white and pink • Super fine weight mohair yarn in white *(for the ear detail)* • B-1 / 2.25 mm crochet hook • Safety eyes (12 mm) • White sewing thread *(for the whiskers)* • Black, pink, green and blue embroidery thread • Yarn needle • Pins • Stitch markers • Fiberfill for stuffing • Optional: super fine weight mohair yarn in white and pink *(if you decide to crochet using two strands of yarn)* • Optional: approx. 4" / 10 cm of wire or pipe cleaner *(for the tail if you want it to be posable)*

NOTE

To achieve the soft texture shown in the photos, I crocheted with two strands held together: one strand of sport weight cotton and one strand of super fine weight mohair in a matching color. This is completely optional, using a single strand of yarn works just as well.

HEAD (in white yarn)
Rnd 1: start 6 sc in a magic ring [6]
Rnd 2: inc in all 6 st [12]
Rnd 3: (sc in next st, inc in next st) repeat 6 times [18]
Rnd 4: (sc in next st, inc in next st, sc in next st) repeat 6 times [24]
Rnd 5: (sc in next 3 st, inc in next st) repeat 6 times [30]
Rnd 6: (sc in next 2 st, inc in next st, sc in next 2 st) repeat 6 times [36]
Rnd 7: (sc in next 5 st, inc in next st) repeat 6 times [42]
Rnd 8: (sc in next 3 st, inc in next st, sc in next 3 st) repeat 6 times [48]
Rnd 9 – 16: sc in all 48 st [48]
Rnd 17: (sc in next 3 st, dec, sc in next 3 st) repeat 6 times [42]
Rnd 18: (sc in next 5 st, dec) repeat 6 times [36]
Insert the safety eyes between rounds 13 and 14, with an interspace of 8 stitches. Stuff the head with fiberfill and continue stuffing as you go.
Rnd 19: (sc in next 2 st, dec, sc in next 2 st) repeat 6 times [30]
Rnd 20: (sc in next 3 st, dec) repeat 6 times [24]
Rnd 21 – 22: sc in all 24 st [24]
Rnd 23: (sc in next 3 st, inc in next st) repeat 6 times [30]
Fasten off, leaving a yarn tail for sewing ❶.

RIGHT EAR

Inner part (in pink yarn)
Ch 2. Crochet in rows.
Row 1: start in second ch from hook, inc in this ch, ch 1, turn [2]
Row 2: sc in next st, inc in next st, ch 1, turn [3]
Row 3: sc in next 2 st, inc in next st, ch 2, turn [4]
Row 4: dc inc in next st, hdc in next st, sc in next 2 st, ch 1, turn [5]

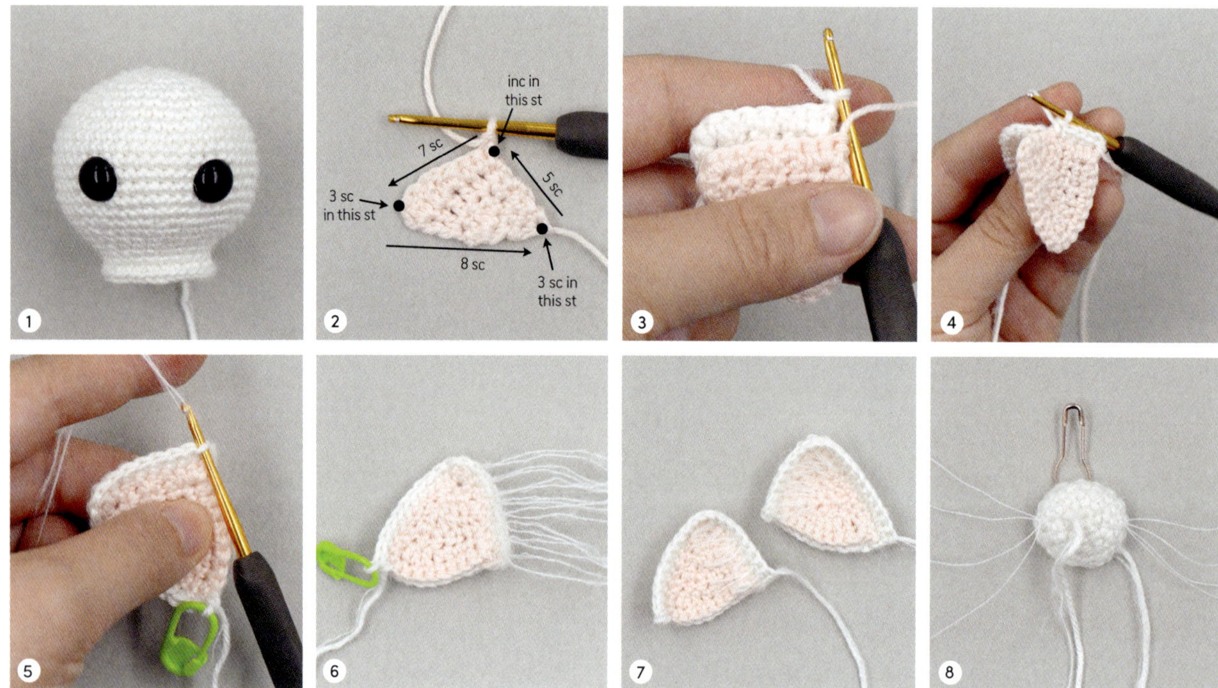

Row 5: sc in next 2 st, hdc in next st, dc in next st, dc inc in next st, ch 2, turn [6]
Row 6: dc inc in next st, dc in next st, hdc inc in next st, sc in next 3 st [8]
Next, we crochet around the ear 2.
Row 7: ch 1, turn, sc in next 7 st, 3 sc in next st, continue in the row-ends on the longer side of the ear, sc in next 8 st, 3 sc in next st, continue in the row-ends on the shorter side of the ear, sc in next 5 st, inc in next st [28]
Fasten off and set aside.

Outer part (in white yarn)
Ch 2. Crochet in rows.
Row 1 – 7: repeat the instructions for the inner part, but don't fasten off.
In the next row, we'll join the inner and outer parts together.
Row 8: ch 1, turn, place the inner part on top of your work with the wrong side facing up and crochet through both layers 3 4, sc in next 20 st, ch 1, turn [20] Leave the remaining stitches unworked.
Pause your work. In the next row, we add a fluffy detail to the ears. Cut 8 strands of white mohair yarn. Attach those strands to the front loops of the first 8 stitches of Row 8, one strand to each stitch 5 6.
Row 9: sc in all 20 st [20]
Fasten off, leaving a whiet yarn tail for sewing. Weave in all other yarn ends. Cut the mohair threads to the desired length.

LEFT EAR

Inner part (in pink yarn)
Ch 2. Crochet in rows.
Row 1: start in second ch from hook, inc in this ch, ch 1, turn [2]
Row 2: sc in next st, inc in next st, ch 1, turn [3]
Row 3: sc in next 2 st, inc in next st, ch 1, turn [4]
Row 4: sc in next 2 st, hdc in next st, dc inc in next st, ch 2, turn [5]
Row 5: dc inc in next st, dc in next st, hdc in next st, sc in next

2 st, ch 1, turn [6]
Row 6: sc in next 3 st, hdc inc in next st, dc in next st, dc inc in next st [8]
Next, we crochet around the ear.
Row 7: ch 1, turn, sc in next 7 st, 3 sc in next st, continue in the row-ends on the shorter side of the ear, sc in next 5 st, 3 sc in next st, continue in the row-ends on the longer side of the ear, sc in next 8 st, inc in next st [28]
Fasten off and set aside.

Outer part (in white yarn)
Ch 2. Crochet in rows.
Row 1 – 7: repeat the instructions for the inner part, but don't fasten off.
In the next row, we'll join the inner and outer parts together.
Row 8: ch 1, turn, place the inner part on top of your work with the wrong side facing up and crochet through both layers, sc in next 20 st, ch 1, turn [20] Leave the remaining stitches unworked.
Pause your work. In the next row, we add a fluffy detail to the ears. Cut 8 strands of white mohair yarn. Attach those strands to the front loops of the last 8 stitches of Row 8, one strand to each stitch.
Row 9: sc in all 20 st [20]
Fasten off, leaving a white yarn tail for sewing. Weave in all other yarn ends (7). Cut the mohair threads to the desired length.

SNOUT (in white yarn)
Rnd 1: start 7 sc in a magic ring [7]
Rnd 2: inc in all 7 st [14]
Rnd 3: sc in next 10 st, hdc inc in next st, dc in next 3 st [15]
Rnd 4: dc in next 2 st, hdc inc in next st, sc in next 4 st *(mark the last sc with a stitch marker),* sc in next 5 st [13] Leave the remaining stitches unworked.
Fasten off, leaving a yarn tail for sewing

Attach the whiskers:
Prepare 4 strands of white sewing thread, each about 6" / 15 cm long. Note that the marked stitch indicates the top center of

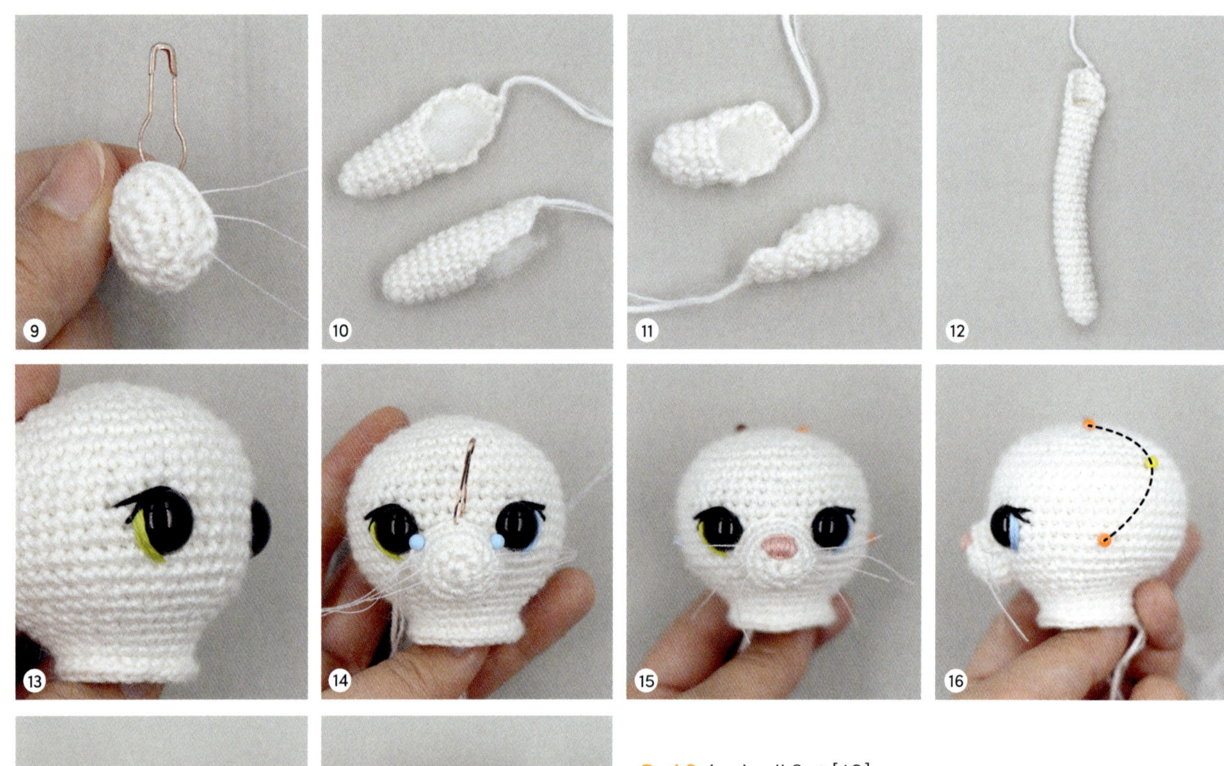

the snout. With the wrong side of the snout facing you, tie 2 strands on the left and 2 strands on the right, keeping the knots on the inside so they remain hidden from the front 8. Each knot creates 2 loose ends, giving you 4 strands on each side. Pull each strand through a separate stitch gap to the front side of the snout 9.

BODY (in white yarn)

Rnd 1: start 6 sc in a magic ring [6]
Rnd 2: inc in all 6 st [12]
Rnd 3: (sc in next st, inc in next st) repeat 6 times [18]
Rnd 4: (sc in next st, inc in next st, sc in next st) repeat 6 times [24]
Rnd 5: (sc in next 3 st, inc in next st) repeat 6 times [30]
Rnd 6: (sc in next 2 st, inc in next st, sc in next 2 st) repeat 6 times [36]
Rnd 7 – 12: sc in all 36 st [36]
Rnd 13: (sc in next 5 st, inc in next st) repeat 6 times [42]
Rnd 14: (sc in next 9 st, inc in next st, sc in next 4 st) repeat 3 times [45]
Rnd 15: (sc in next 14 st, inc in next st) repeat 3 times [48]
Rnd 16 – 19: sc in all 48 st [48]
Stuff the body with fiberfill and continue stuffing as you go.
Rnd 20: (sc in next 3 st, dec, sc in next 3 st) repeat 6 times [42]
Rnd 21: (sc in next 5 st, dec) repeat 6 times [36]
Rnd 22: (sc in next 2 st, dec, sc in next 2 st) repeat 6 times [30]
Rnd 23: (sc in next 3 st, dec) repeat 6 times [24]
Rnd 24: (sc in next st, dec, sc in next st) repeat 6 times [18]

Rnd 25: (sc in next st, dec) repeat 6 times [12]
Rnd 26: dec 6 times [6]
Fasten off, leaving a yarn tail. Using a yarn needle, weave the yarn tail through the front loop of each remaining stitch and pull it tight to close. Weave in the yarn end.

FRONT LEG (make 2, in white yarn)

Rnd 1: start 6 sc in a magic ring [6]
Rnd 2: (sc in next st, inc in next st) repeat 3 times [9]
Rnd 3: sc in next 4 st, inc in next st, sc in next 4 st [10]
Rnd 4: sc in next 9 st, inc in next st [11]
Rnd 5: sc in next 5 st, inc in next st, sc in next 5 st [12]
Rnd 6 – 7: sc in all 12 st [12]
Rnd 8: sc in all 12 st, ch 1, turn [12]
Continue crocheting in rows.
Row 9: skip first sc, sc in next 8 st, ch 1, turn [8] Leave the remaining stitches unworked.
Row 10: skip first sc, sc in next 7 st, ch 1, turn [7]
Row 11: skip first sc, sc in next 6 st, ch 1, turn [6]
Row 12: skip first sc, sc in next 5 st, ch 1, turn [5]
Row 13: skip first sc, sc in next 4 st, ch 1, turn [4]
Row 14: skip first sc, sc in next 3 st [3]
Fasten off, leaving a yarn tail for sewing. Stuff the front legs with fiberfill ⑩.

HIND LEG (make 2)

Foot (in white yarn)

Rnd 1: start 5 sc in a magic ring [5]
Rnd 2: inc in all 5 st [10]
Rnd 3 – 4: sc in all 10 st [10]
Rnd 5: sc in all 10 st, ch 1, turn [10]
Continue crocheting in rows.
Row 6: skip first sc, sc in next 6 st, ch 1, turn [6] Leave the remaining stitches unworked.
Row 7: skip first sc, sc in next 5 st, ch 1, turn [5]
Row 8: skip first sc, sc in next 4 st, ch 1, turn [4]
Row 9: skip first sc, sc in next 3 st [3]
Fasten off, leaving a yarn tail for sewing. Stuff the feet with fiberfill ⑪.

Upper part (in white yarn)

Rnd 1: start 6 sc in a magic ring [6]
Rnd 2: inc in all 6 st [12]
Rnd 3: (sc in next st, inc in next st) repeat 6 times [18]
Rnd 4: (sc in next st, inc in next st, sc in next st) repeat 6 times [24]
Rnd 5: (sc in next 3 st, inc in next st) repeat 6 times [30]
Rnd 6: (sc in next 2 st, inc in next st, sc in next 2 st) repeat 6 times [36]
Fasten off, leaving a yarn tail for sewing.

TAIL (in white yarn)

Rnd 1: start 5 sc in a magic ring [5]
Rnd 2: inc in all 5 st [10]
Rnd 3 – 24: sc in all 10 st [10]
Rnd 25: sc in all 10 st, ch 1, turn [10]
Continue crocheting in rows.
Row 26: skip first sc, sc in next 6 st, ch 1, turn [6] Leave the remaining stitches unworked.
Row 27: skip first sc, sc in next 5 st, ch 1, turn [5]
Row 28: skip first sc, sc in next 4 st, ch 1, turn [4]
Row 29: skip first sc, sc in next 3 st [3]
Fasten off, leaving a yarn tail for sewing ⑫.

ASSEMBLY

Make the eyes colorful

- Using several strands of thread, embroider a line along the outer edge of each eye ⑬. One eye should be blue and the other one green.
- Using black thread, embroider the upper outline and eyelashes ⑬.

Attach the snout

- Position the snout just below the eyes, with the stitch marker centered between them ⑭. Pin it in place, remove the stitch marker and sew around using the remaining yarn tail. Stuff the snout with fiberfill before closing the seam.
- Using pink thread, embroider a nose on round 2 of the top side of the snout.

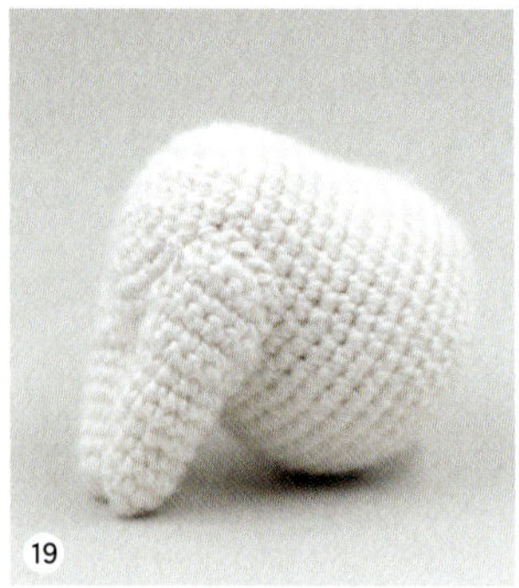
19

20

21

22

- Cut the whiskers to the desired length. You get the cutest look when each whisker is a slightly different length 15.

Attach the ears

- Position the ears on both sides of the head, between rounds 3-14 16 17. Pin them in place and sew them on using the remaining yarn tails 18.

Attach the front legs

- Place the front legs on the upper (narrow) side of the body, on rounds 5-10 of the body. The longer edges of the legs should face outward. Pin them in place and sew around using the remaining yarn tails 19.

Attach the hind legs

- Place the upper parts of the hind legs on the lower sides of the body. It's easiest to do this while your cat is sitting on a flat surface. The upper parts should be on rounds 12-23 of the body. Pin them in place and sew around using the remaining yarn tails. Add some stuffing before closing the seam 20.
- Place the feet below the upper parts of the hind legs. The feet should be facing the front side of the cat. Pin them in place and sew around using the remaining yarn tails 21 22.

Attach the head

- Place the head on top of the body, it should cover rounds 2-10 of the body. Turn the head slightly to the side to give your cat a cuter look. Pin it in place and sew around using the remaining yarn tail.

Attach the tail

- If you want the tail to be posable, insert the wire or pipe cleaner. Otherwise, lightly stuff it with fiberfill.
- Position the tail to the back of the body, with the tail pointing to the same side your cat is looking at. Pin it in place and sew around using the remaining yarn tail.
- Slightly bend the tail upward to give your cat a cuter look.